THE 100+ SERIES™

Reproducible Activities

Geometry

Grades 5–8

By
Mary Lee Vivian
Tammy Bohn-Voepel
Margaret Thomas

Published by Instructional Fair • TS Denison
an imprint of

Mc Graw Hill **Children's Publishing**

Author: Mary Lee Vivian, Tammy Bohn-Voepel, Margaret Thomas
Editor: Jerry Aten

 **Children's Publishing**

Published by Instructional Fair • TS Denison
An imprint of McGraw-Hill Children's Publishing
Copyright © 2003 McGraw-Hill Children's Publishing

Send all inquiries to:
McGraw-Hill Children's Publishing
3195 Wilson Drive NW
Grand Rapids, Michigan 49544

Geometry—grades 5-8
ISBN: 0-7424-1776-X

3 4 5 6 7 8 9 PHXBK 08 07 06 05 04

NCTM Standards of Math for Grades 5–8

Note to Teacher: Each activity in this book has been linked to the related NCTM Standards listed below. The numbers of the related Standards for each activity are indicated in the Table of Contents.

1. Number and Operations – Understand numbers, ways of representing numbers, relationships among numbers, and number systems. Understand meanings of operations and how they relate to one another. Compute fluently and make reasonable estimates.

2. Algebra – Understand patterns, relations, and functions. Represent and analyze mathematical situations and structures using algebraic symbols. Use mathematical models to represent and understand quantitative relationships. Analyze change in various contexts.

3. Geometry – Analyze characteristics and properties of two- and three-dimensional geometric shapes and develop mathematical arguments about geometric relationships. Specify locations and describe spatial relationships using coordinate geometry and other representational systems. Apply transformations and use symmetry to analyze mathematical situations. Use visualization, spatial reasoning, and geometric modeling to solve problems.

4. Measurement – Understand measurable attributes of objects and the units, systems, and processes of measurement. Apply appropriate techniques, tools, and formulas to determine measurements.

5. Data Analysis and Probability – Formulate questions that can be addressed with data and collect, organize, and display relevant data to answer them. Select and use appropriate statistical methods to analyze data. Develop and evaluate inferences and predictions that are based on data. Understand and apply basic concepts of probability.

6. Problem Solving – Build new mathematical knowledge through problem solving. Solve problems that arise in mathematics and in other contexts. Apply and adapt a variety of appropriate strategies to solve problems. Monitor and reflect on the process of mathematical problem solving.

7. Reasoning and Proof – Recognize reasoning and proof as fundamental aspects of mathematics. Make and investigate mathematical conjectures. Develop and evaluate mathematical arguments and proofs. Select and use various types of reasoning and methods of proof.

8. Communication – Organize and consolidate their mathematical thinking through communication. Communicate their mathematical thinking coherently and clearly to peers, teachers, and others. Analyze and evaluate the mathematical thinking and strategies of others. Use the language of mathematics to express mathematical ideas precisely.

9. Connections – Recognize and use connections among mathematical ideas. Understand how mathematical ideas interconnect and build on one another to produce a coherent whole. Recognize and apply mathematics in contexts outside of mathematics.

10. Representation – Create and use representations to organize, record, and communicate mathematical ideas. Select, apply, and translate among mathematical representations to solve problems. Use representations to model and interpret physical, social, and mathematical phenomena.

Table of Contents

Name _____   Date _____

Length, Links, and Midpoint Magic

Find the length of segment $\overline{FM}$.
$$\overline{FM} = |^-5 - 2| = |^-7| = 7$$
Find the coordinate of the midpoint of segment $\overline{IO}$.
$$\text{Midpoint} = \frac{(^-2 + 4)}{2} = 1$$

A B C D E F G H I J K L M N O P Q R S T U V W

$^-10$ $^-9$ $^-8$ $^-7$ $^-6$ $^-5$ $^-4$ $^-3$ $^-2$ $^-1$ 0 1 2 3 4 5 6 7 8 9 10 11 12

Find the length of each segment and link the segments in Columns A and B that have equal lengths.

Column A
1. Segment $\overline{GW}$
2. Segment $\overline{BN}$
3. Segment $\overline{PV}$
4. Segment $\overline{KR}$
5. Segment with endpoints $\frac{3}{4}$ and $5\frac{3}{4}$
6. Segment with endpoints $^-3$ and $^-7\frac{1}{2}$
7. Segment with endpoints $-\frac{1}{4}$ and $3\frac{1}{4}$
8. Segment with endpoints $\frac{1}{4}$ and $3\frac{1}{4}$

Column B
A. Segment $\overline{EL}$
B. Segment $\overline{AF}$
C. Segment $\overline{CS}$
D. Segment $\overline{MS}$
E. Segment with endpoints $^-2$ and 10
F. Segment with endpoints $^-1\frac{1}{2}$ and 3
G. Segment with endpoints $^-1\frac{3}{4}$ and $1\frac{3}{4}$
H. Segment with endpoints $^-5$ and $^-2$

In a Magic Square, each row, column, and diagonal has the same: Magic Sum. Find the length of the segments and determine the Magic Sum: _____.

Endpoints $1\frac{1}{2}$ and 2	Endpoints $^-3$ and $4\frac{1}{2}$	Segment $\overline{DK}$	Segment $\overline{HJ}$
Segment $\overline{HN}$	Segment $\overline{QT}$	Endpoints $6\frac{1}{2}$ and 3	Endpoints $5\frac{3}{4}$ and $1\frac{1}{4}$
Segment $\overline{DH}$	Segment $\overline{JO}$	Endpoints $1\frac{3}{4}$ and $^-3\frac{3}{4}$	Endpoints $1\frac{1}{2}$ and $^-1$
Endpoints $^-2\frac{1}{4}$ and $4\frac{1}{4}$	Endpoints $^-5\frac{1}{2}$ and $^-4$	Segment $\overline{JK}$	Segment $\overline{AI}$

0-7424-1776-X *Geometry*

Congruence of Segments and Addition Properties

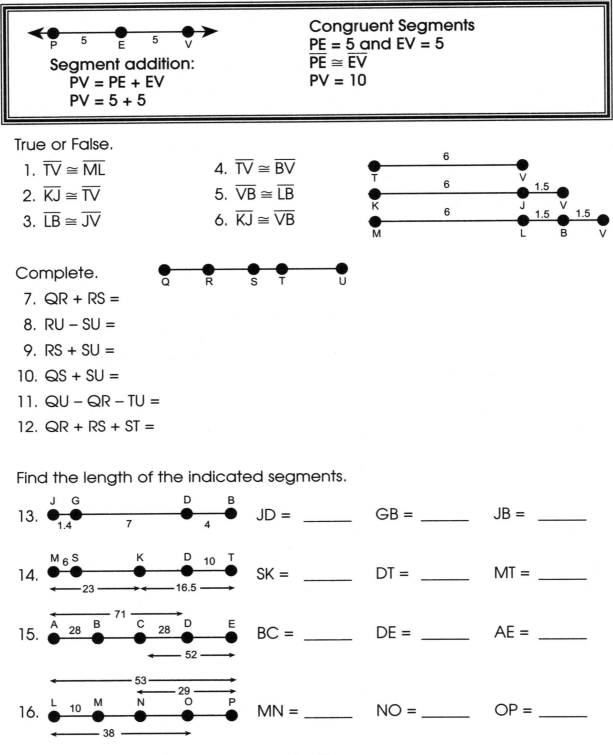

Segment addition:
PV = PE + EV
PV = 5 + 5

Congruent Segments
PE = 5 and EV = 5
$\overline{PE} \cong \overline{EV}$
PV = 10

True or False.

1. $\overline{TV} \cong \overline{ML}$ 4. $\overline{TV} \cong \overline{BV}$

2. $\overline{KJ} \cong \overline{TV}$ 5. $\overline{VB} \cong \overline{LB}$

3. $\overline{LB} \cong \overline{JV}$ 6. $\overline{KJ} \cong \overline{VB}$

Complete.

7. QR + RS =

8. RU – SU =

9. RS + SU =

10. QS + SU =

11. QU – QR – TU =

12. QR + RS + ST =

Find the length of the indicated segments.

13.   JD = _____   GB = _____   JB = _____

14.   SK = _____   DT = _____   MT = _____

15.   BC = _____   DE = _____   AE = _____

16.   MN = _____   NO = _____   OP = _____

17. Which segments are congruent in #15?

Angles (∠)

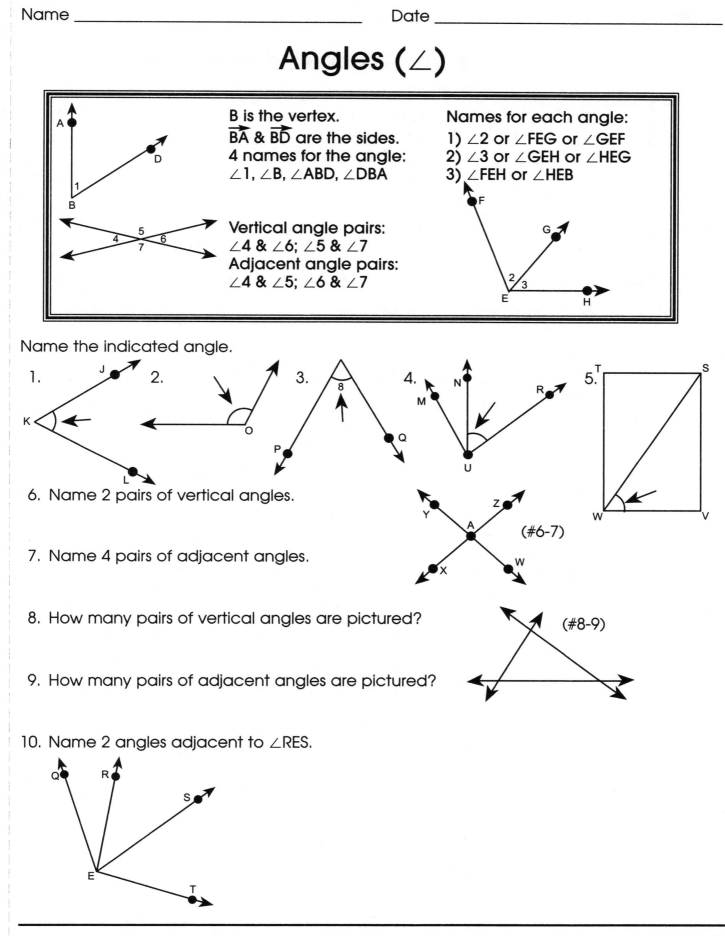

B is the vertex.
$\overrightarrow{BA}$ & $\overrightarrow{BD}$ are the sides.
4 names for the angle:
∠1, ∠B, ∠ABD, ∠DBA

Vertical angle pairs:
∠4 & ∠6; ∠5 & ∠7
Adjacent angle pairs:
∠4 & ∠5; ∠6 & ∠7

Names for each angle:
1) ∠2 or ∠FEG or ∠GEF
2) ∠3 or ∠GEH or ∠HEG
3) ∠FEH or ∠HEB

Name the indicated angle.

1.

2.

3.

4.

5.

6. Name 2 pairs of vertical angles.

7. Name 4 pairs of adjacent angles.

(#6-7)

8. How many pairs of vertical angles are pictured?

(#8-9)

9. How many pairs of adjacent angles are pictured?

10. Name 2 angles adjacent to ∠RES.

Congruence of Angles and Addition Properties

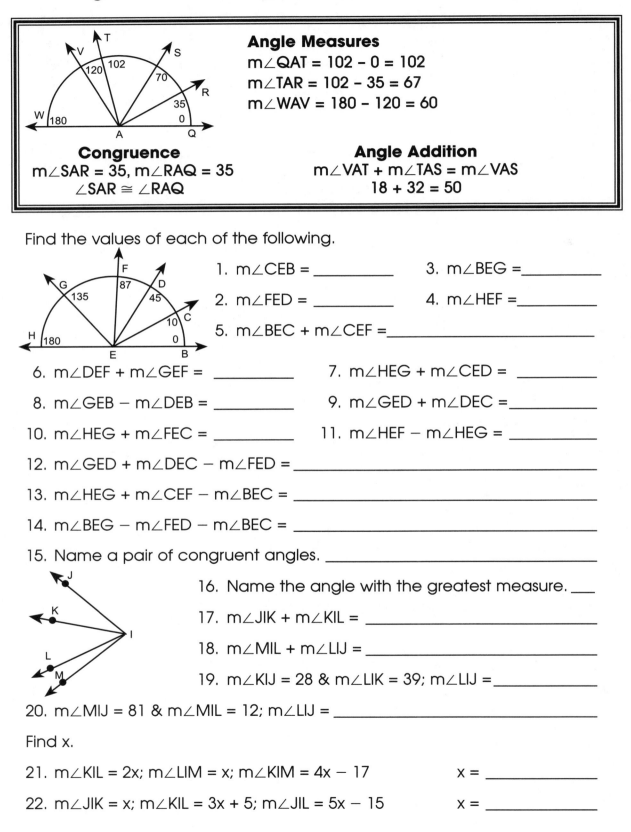

Angle Measures
m∠QAT = 102 – 0 = 102
m∠TAR = 102 – 35 = 67
m∠WAV = 180 – 120 = 60

Congruence
m∠SAR = 35, m∠RAQ = 35
∠SAR ≅ ∠RAQ

Angle Addition
m∠VAT + m∠TAS = m∠VAS
18 + 32 = 50

Find the values of each of the following.

1. m∠CEB = _____

2. m∠FED = _____

3. m∠BEG = _____

4. m∠HEF = _____

5. m∠BEC + m∠CEF = _____

6. m∠DEF + m∠GEF = _____

7. m∠HEG + m∠CED = _____

8. m∠GEB − m∠DEB = _____

9. m∠GED + m∠DEC = _____

10. m∠HEG + m∠FEC = _____

11. m∠HEF − m∠HEG = _____

12. m∠GED + m∠DEC − m∠FED = _____

13. m∠HEG + m∠CEF − m∠BEC = _____

14. m∠BEG − m∠FED − m∠BEC = _____

15. Name a pair of congruent angles. _____

16. Name the angle with the greatest measure. ___

17. m∠JIK + m∠KIL = _____

18. m∠MIL + m∠LIJ = _____

19. m∠KIJ = 28 & m∠LIK = 39; m∠LIJ = _____

20. m∠MIJ = 81 & m∠MIL = 12; m∠LIJ = _____

Find x.

21. m∠KIL = 2x; m∠LIM = x; m∠KIM = 4x − 17   x = _____

22. m∠JIK = x; m∠KIL = 3x + 5; m∠JIL = 5x − 15   x = _____

Classifying Angles

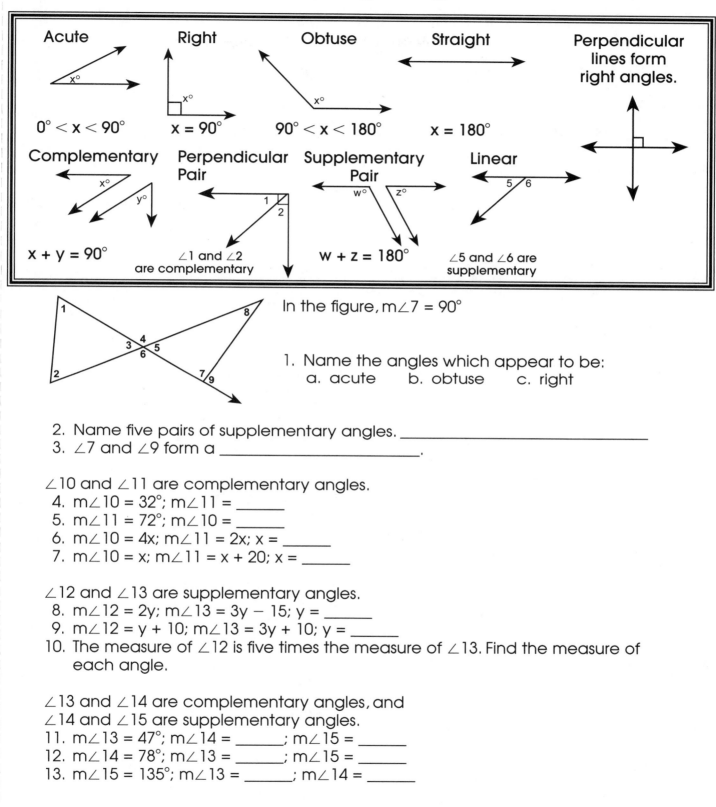

Acute

$0° < x < 90°$

Right

$x = 90°$

Obtuse

$90° < x < 180°$

Straight

$x = 180°$

Perpendicular lines form right angles.

Complementary

$x + y = 90°$

Perpendicular Pair

∠1 and ∠2 are complementary

Supplementary Pair

$w + z = 180°$

Linear

∠5 and ∠6 are supplementary

In the figure, m∠7 = 90°

1. Name the angles which appear to be:
   a. acute   b. obtuse   c. right

2. Name five pairs of supplementary angles. _____

3. ∠7 and ∠9 form a _____ .

∠10 and ∠11 are complementary angles.
   4. m∠10 = 32°; m∠11 = _____
   5. m∠11 = 72°; m∠10 = _____
   6. m∠10 = 4x; m∠11 = 2x; x = _____
   7. m∠10 = x; m∠11 = x + 20; x = _____

∠12 and ∠13 are supplementary angles.
   8. m∠12 = 2y; m∠13 = 3y − 15; y = _____
   9. m∠12 = y + 10; m∠13 = 3y + 10; y = _____
   10. The measure of ∠12 is five times the measure of ∠13. Find the measure of each angle.

∠13 and ∠14 are complementary angles, and ∠14 and ∠15 are supplementary angles.
   11. m∠13 = 47°; m∠14 = _____; m∠15 = _____
   12. m∠14 = 78°; m∠13 = _____; m∠15 = _____
   13. m∠15 = 135°; m∠13 = _____; m∠14 = _____

Mixed Practice with Angles

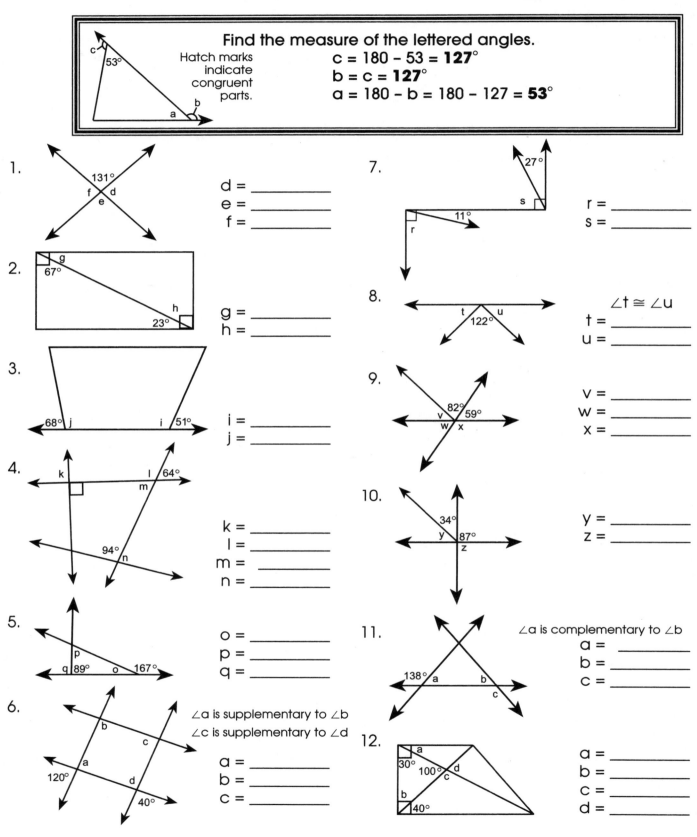

Find the measure of the lettered angles.

Hatch marks indicate congruent parts.

$c = 180 - 53 = \mathbf{127°}$
$b = c = \mathbf{127°}$
$a = 180 - b = 180 - 127 = \mathbf{53°}$

1.
131°
d = _____
e = _____
f = _____

2.
67°
23°
g = _____
h = _____

3.
68° 51°
i = _____
j = _____

4.
64°
94°
k = _____
l = _____
m = _____
n = _____

5.
89° 167°
o = _____
p = _____
q = _____

6.
120°
40°
∠a is supplementary to ∠b
∠c is supplementary to ∠d
a = _____
b = _____
c = _____

7.
27°
11°
r = _____
s = _____

8.
122°
∠t ≅ ∠u
t = _____
u = _____

9.
82° 59°
v = _____
w = _____
x = _____

10.
34° 87°
y = _____
z = _____

11.
138°
∠a is complementary to ∠b
a = _____
b = _____
c = _____

12.
30° 100°
40°
a = _____
b = _____
c = _____
d = _____

Algebra Applications with Angles

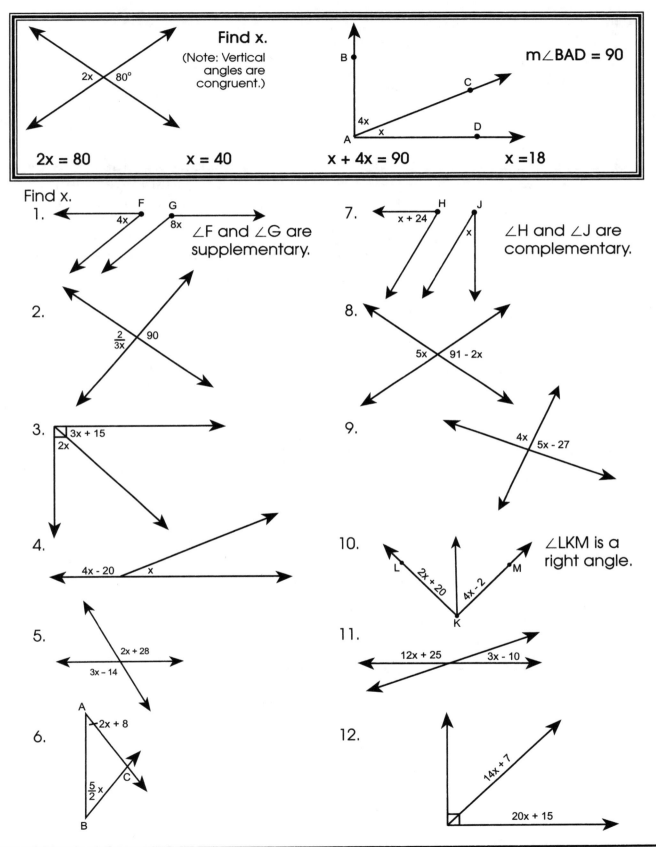

Find x.
(Note: Vertical angles are congruent.)

2x   80°

m∠BAD = 90

B
C
4x
x
A   D

2x = 80   x = 40   x + 4x = 90   x = 18

Find x.

1. F G
   4x 8x   ∠F and ∠G are supplementary.

2.   2/3x 90

3. 3x + 15
    2x

4. 4x - 20   x

5. 2x + 28
    3x – 14

6. A
    2x + 8
    C
    5/2 x
    B

7. H J
    x + 24 x   ∠H and ∠J are complementary.

8. 5x 91 – 2x

9. 4x 5x - 27

10. L M
    2x + 20 4x - 2   ∠LKM is a right angle.
    K

11. 12x + 25   3x - 10

12. 14x + 7
    20x + 15

Triangles (△)

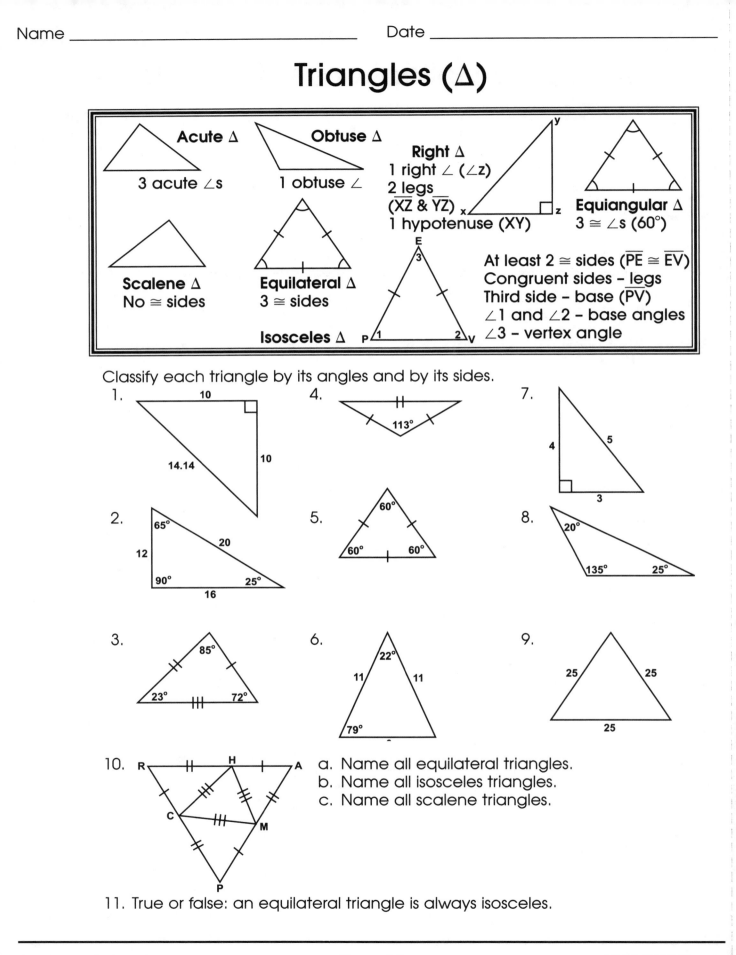

Classify each triangle by its angles and by its sides.

1. 10, 14.14, 10 (right angle)

2. 65°, 20, 12, 90°, 25°, 16

3. 85°, 23°, 72°

4. 113°

5. 60°, 60°, 60°

6. 22°, 11, 11, 79°

7. 4, 5, 3 (right angle)

8. 20°, 135°, 25°

9. 25, 25, 25

10. R, H, A, C, M, P

a. Name all equilateral triangles.
b. Name all isosceles triangles.
c. Name all scalene triangles.

11. True or false: an equilateral triangle is always isosceles.

Congruence of Triangles

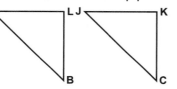

Corresponding Parts ≅

$\overline{AB} \cong \overline{DE}$ $\angle A \cong \angle D$

$\overline{BC} \cong \overline{EF}$ $\angle B \cong \angle E$

$\overline{AC} \cong \overline{DF}$ $\angle C \cong \angle F$

$\triangle ABC \cong \triangle DEF$

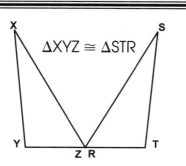

$\triangle XYZ \cong \triangle STR$

1. Name 3 pairs of congruent angles.
2. Name 3 pairs of congruent sides.

Which statements appear to be true?

3. $\angle SLB \cong \angle JKC$ 6. $\angle SLB \cong \angle CJK$
4. $\angle LBS \cong \angle JCK$ 7. $\angle SBL \cong \angle JCK$
5. $\angle SLB \cong \angle CKJ$ 8. $\angle BLS \cong \angle JKC$

For the given congruence, list the six pairs of congruent parts.

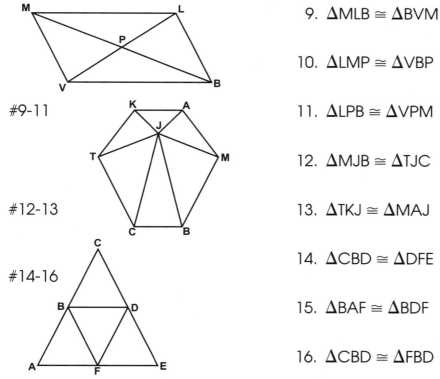

#9-11

#12-13

#14-16

9. $\triangle MLB \cong \triangle BVM$

10. $\triangle LMP \cong \triangle VBP$

11. $\triangle LPB \cong \triangle VPM$

12. $\triangle MJB \cong \triangle TJC$

13. $\triangle TKJ \cong \triangle MAJ$

14. $\triangle CBD \cong \triangle DFE$

15. $\triangle BAF \cong \triangle BDF$

16. $\triangle CBD \cong \triangle FBD$

Symmetry

Symmetry is a type of balance some figures have. If these figures are moved in a specified way, the image will coincide with the figure.

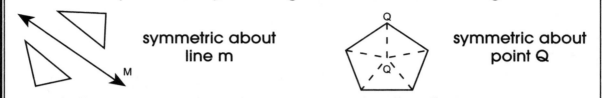

symmetric about line m

symmetric about point Q

Identify the following as symmetric or not symmetric.

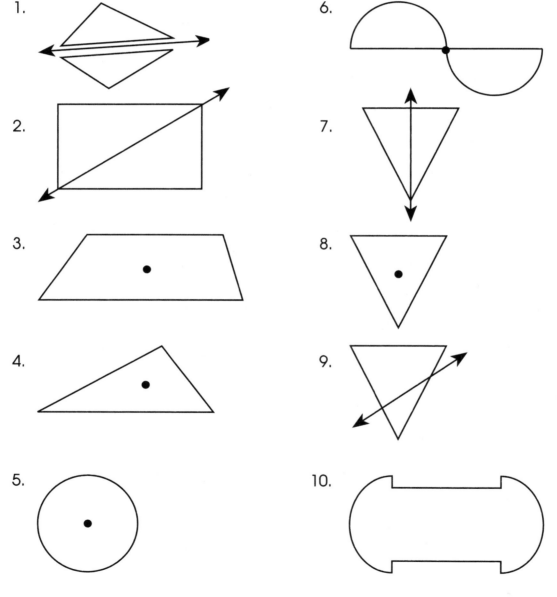

1.

2.

3.

4.

5.

6.

7.

8.

9.

10.

0-7424-1776-X *Geometry*

Orientation

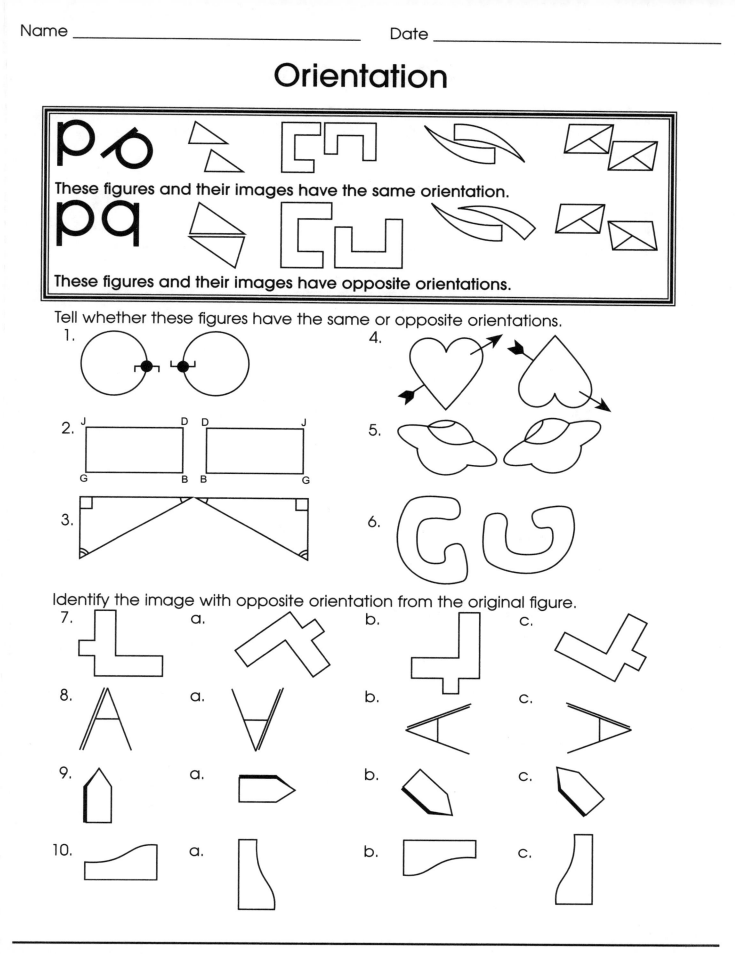

These figures and their images have the same orientation.

These figures and their images have opposite orientations.

Tell whether these figures have the same or opposite orientations.

1.

2.

3.

4.

5.

6.

Identify the image with opposite orientation from the original figure.

7.   a.   b.   c.

8.   a.   b.   c.

9.   a.   b.   c.

10.   a.   b.   c.

Reflections

A **reflection** requires a flip. The original figure and its image have oppo-site orientations.

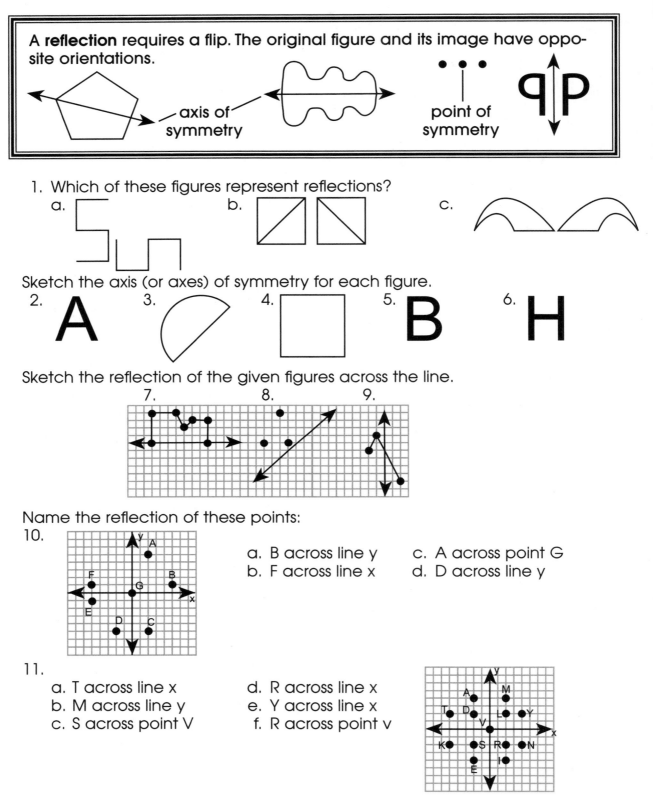

axis of symmetry

point of symmetry

1. Which of these figures represent reflections?

   a.   b.   c.

Sketch the axis (or axes) of symmetry for each figure.

2. A   3. ◠   4. ☐   5. B   6. H

Sketch the reflection of the given figures across the line.

7.   8.   9.

Name the reflection of these points:

10.

a. B across line y   c. A across point G
b. F across line x   d. D across line y

11.

a. T across line x   d. R across line x
b. M across line y   e. Y across line x
c. S across point V   f. R across point v

Rotations

A **rotation** is a turn about a point. The original figure and its image have the same orientation.

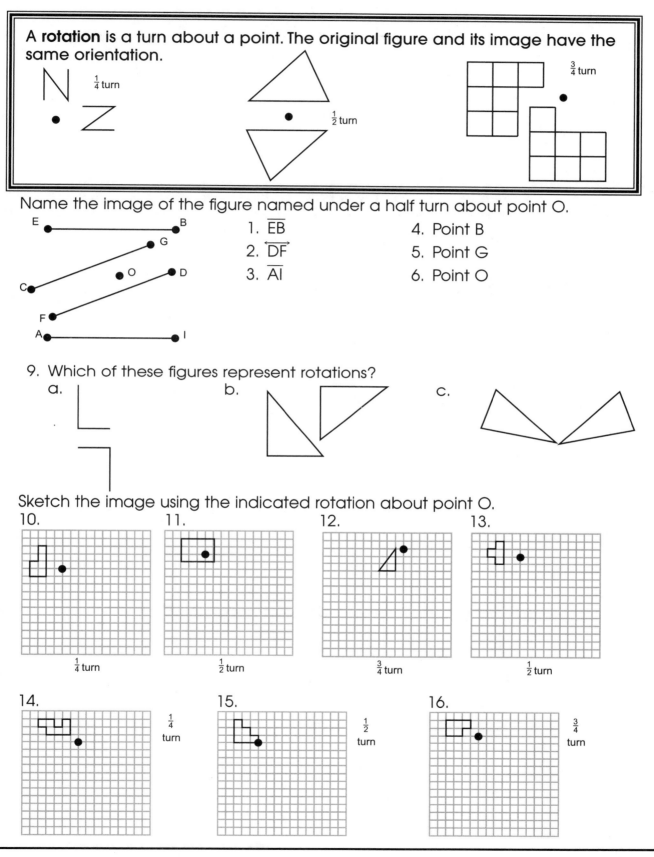

Name the image of the figure named under a half turn about point O.

1. $\overline{EB}$
2. $\overleftrightarrow{DF}$
3. $\overline{AI}$

4. Point B
5. Point G
6. Point O

9. Which of these figures represent rotations?

a.

b.

c.

Sketch the image using the indicated rotation about point O.

10.

$\frac{1}{4}$ turn

11.

$\frac{1}{2}$ turn

12.

$\frac{3}{4}$ turn

13.

$\frac{1}{2}$ turn

14.

$\frac{1}{4}$ turn

15.

$\frac{1}{2}$ turn

16.

$\frac{3}{4}$ turn

Translations

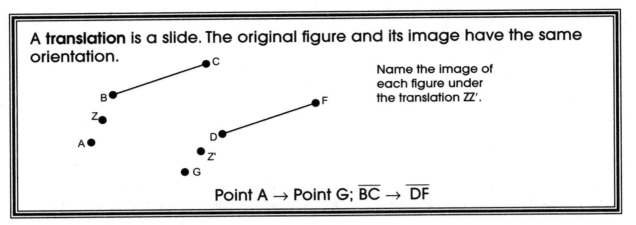

A **translation** is a slide. The original figure and its image have the same orientation.

Name the image of each figure under the translation ZZ'.

Point A → Point G; $\overline{BC}$ → $\overline{DF}$

1. Which of these figures represent translations?

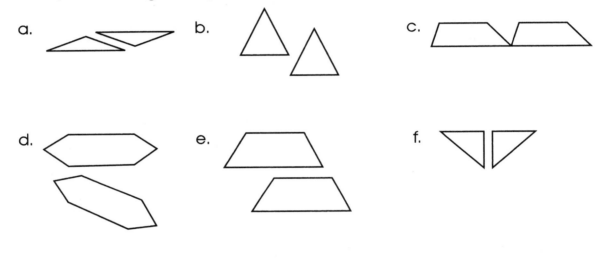

a.   b.   c.

d.   e.   f.

Name the image of each figure under the translation EE'.

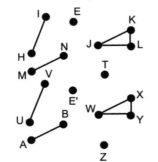

2. Point T   5. Point N

3. $\overline{MN}$ 6. $\overline{HI}$

4. ΔJKL   7. Point H

Mixed Practice with Transformations

A c E H o R S T w X Z

1-5. Sketch each letter which is point symmetric and mark the point of symmetry.

6-13. Sketch each letter that is line symmetric and draw **all** lines of symmetry.

Each of these figures has been moved in a series of basic motions. Name the motion indicated by the lettered arrow.

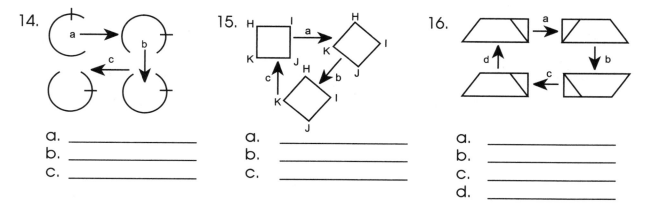

14.

a. _____
b. _____
c. _____

15.

a. _____
b. _____
c. _____

16.

a. _____
b. _____
c. _____
d. _____

Tell which single basic motion will make these figures coincide.

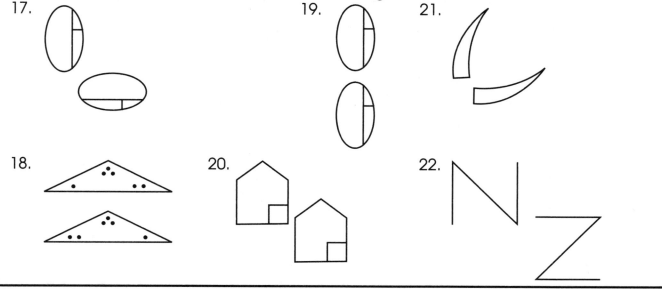

17.

18.

19.

20.

21.

22.

Transformations with Dots and Graphs

1. Draw the reflection of △MSD around the line ℓ and label it M'S'D'; draw one half turn rotation around point P and label it M"S"D".

2. Find the image of each figure using the translation KK'.

More Transformations with Dots and Graphs

For each point named, give its reflection across the

    a. x-axis   b. origin   c. y-axis

1. (2, ⁻3)

2. (⁻4, ⁻1)

3. (5, 5)

4. (⁻1, 2)

5. (a, b)

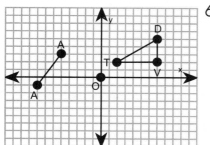

6. Find the image of $\triangle$TDV:

    a. for the rotation of a $\frac{1}{4}$ turn counterclockwise.

    b. for the translation AA′.

    c. for the reflection across O.

7. Find the image of QRST:

    a. for the reflection across the x-axis.

    b. for the rotation about O of a $\frac{1}{2}$ turn clockwise.

    c. for the translation of BB′.

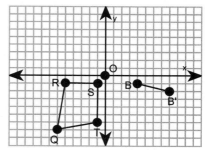

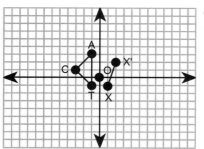

8. Find the image of $\triangle$CAT:

    a. for the reflection across the y-axis.

    b. for the translation XX′.

    c. for the rotation about O of a $\frac{3}{4}$ turn clockwise.

Included Sides and Angles

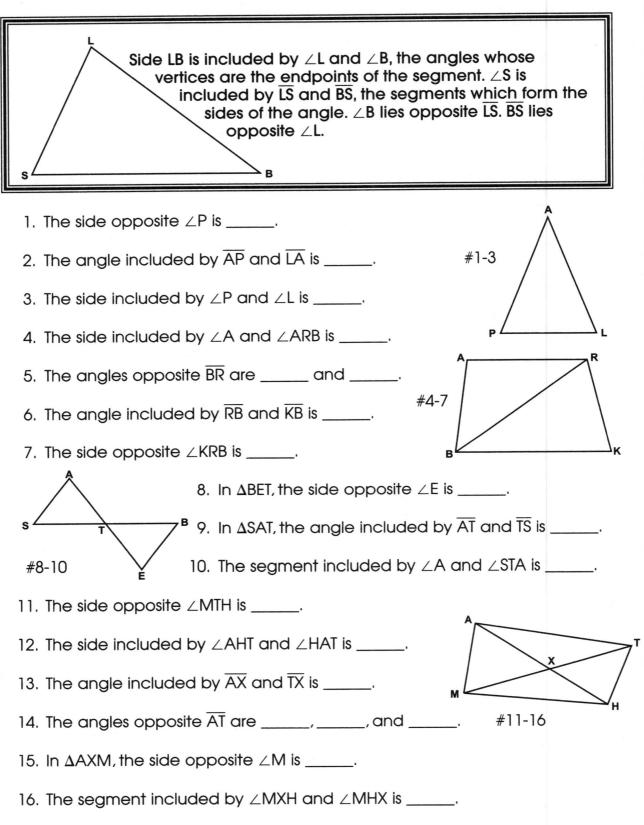

Side LB is included by ∠L and ∠B, the angles whose vertices are the endpoints of the segment. ∠S is included by $\overline{LS}$ and $\overline{BS}$, the segments which form the sides of the angle. ∠B lies opposite $\overline{LS}$. $\overline{BS}$ lies opposite ∠L.

1. The side opposite ∠P is _____.

2. The angle included by $\overline{AP}$ and $\overline{LA}$ is _____.   #1-3

3. The side included by ∠P and ∠L is _____.

4. The side included by ∠A and ∠ARB is _____.

5. The angles opposite $\overline{BR}$ are _____ and _____.   #4-7

6. The angle included by $\overline{RB}$ and $\overline{KB}$ is _____.

7. The side opposite ∠KRB is _____.

8. In △BET, the side opposite ∠E is _____.

9. In △SAT, the angle included by $\overline{AT}$ and $\overline{TS}$ is _____.

#8-10   10. The segment included by ∠A and ∠STA is _____.

11. The side opposite ∠MTH is _____.

12. The side included by ∠AHT and ∠HAT is _____.

13. The angle included by $\overline{AX}$ and $\overline{TX}$ is _____.

14. The angles opposite $\overline{AT}$ are _____, _____, and _____.   #11-16

15. In △AXM, the side opposite ∠M is _____.

16. The segment included by ∠MXH and ∠MHX is _____.

Ways to Prove Triangles Congruent

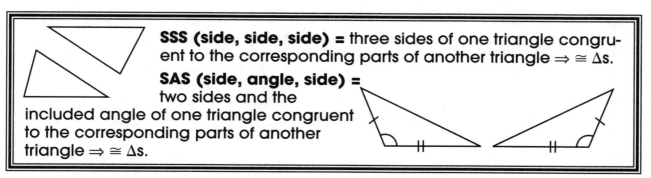

SSS (side, side, side) = three sides of one triangle congruent to the corresponding parts of another triangle ⟹ ≅ Δs.

SAS (side, angle, side) =
two sides and the
included angle of one triangle congruent
to the corresponding parts of another
triangle ⟹ ≅ Δs.

Identify which property will prove these triangles congruent (SSS, SAS, or none).

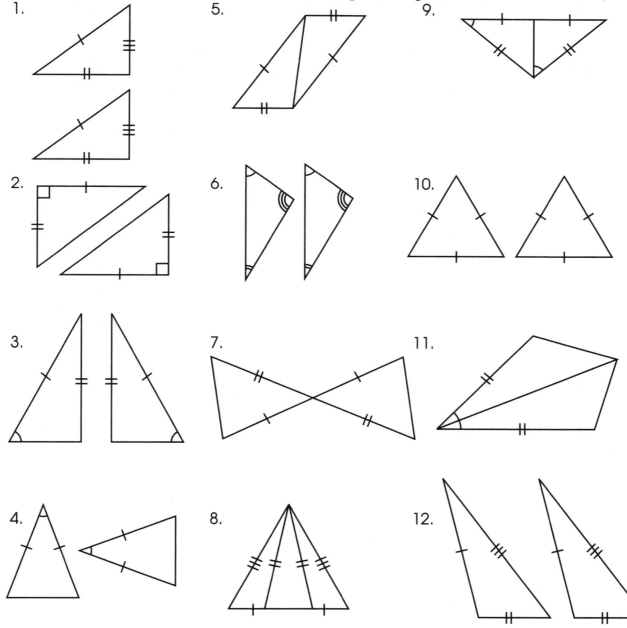

1.

2.

3.

4.

5.

6.

7.

8.

9.

10.

11.

12.

More Ways to Prove Triangles Congruent

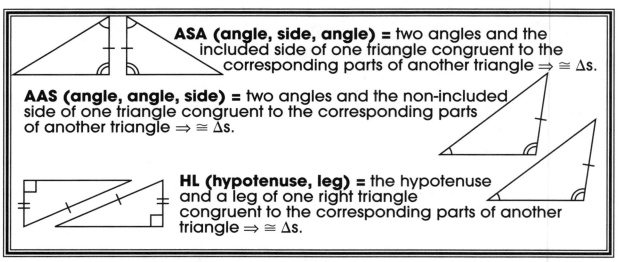

ASA (angle, side, angle) = two angles and the included side of one triangle congruent to the corresponding parts of another triangle $\Rightarrow\ \cong \Delta$s.

AAS (angle, angle, side) = two angles and the non-included side of one triangle congruent to the corresponding parts of another triangle $\Rightarrow\ \cong \Delta$s.

HL (hypotenuse, leg) = the hypotenuse and a leg of one right triangle congruent to the corresponding parts of another triangle $\Rightarrow\ \cong \Delta$s.

Identify which property will prove these triangles congruent (ASA, AAS, HL or none).

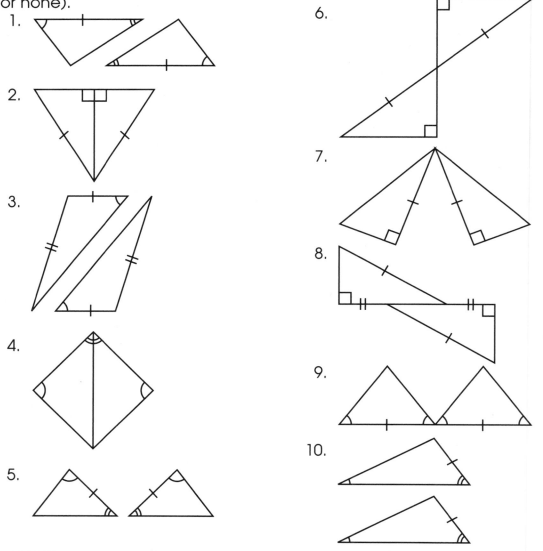

1.

2.

3.

4.

5.

6.

7.

8.

9.

10.

More Congruent Triangles

Identify which property will prove these triangles congruent (SSS, SAS, ASA, AAS, HL or none).

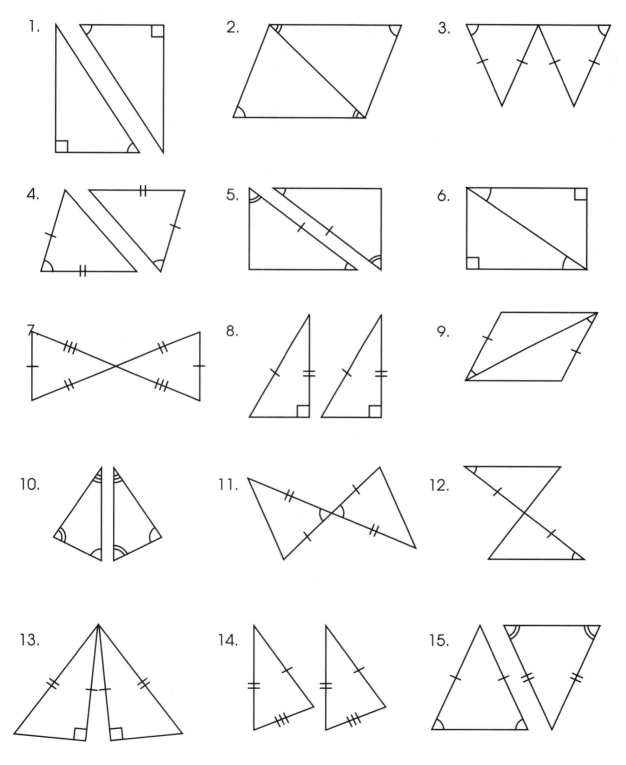

Triangle Inequality Properties

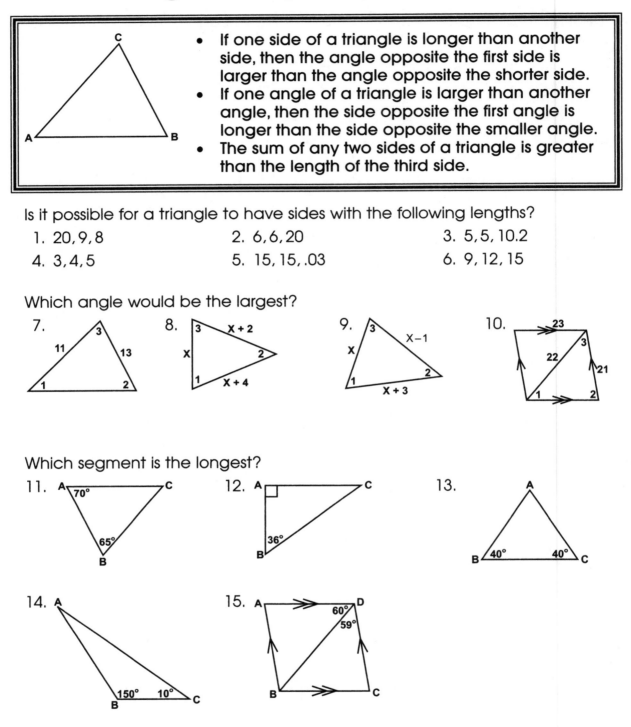

- If one side of a triangle is longer than another side, then the angle opposite the first side is larger than the angle opposite the shorter side.
- If one angle of a triangle is larger than another angle, then the side opposite the first angle is longer than the side opposite the smaller angle.
- The sum of any two sides of a triangle is greater than the length of the third side.

Is it possible for a triangle to have sides with the following lengths?

1. 20, 9, 8

2. 6, 6, 20

3. 5, 5, 10.2

4. 3, 4, 5

5. 15, 15, .03

6. 9, 12, 15

Which angle would be the largest?

7.

8.

9.

10.

Which segment is the longest?

11.

12.

13.

14.

15.

Proofs in Column Form

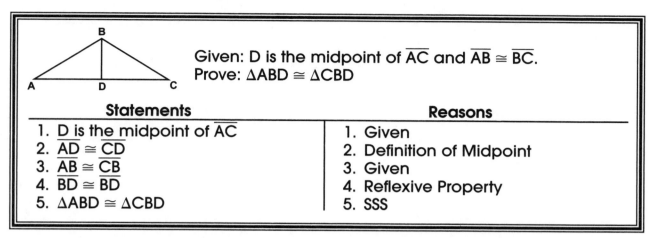

Given: D is the midpoint of $\overline{AC}$ and $\overline{AB} \cong \overline{BC}$.
Prove: $\triangle ABD \cong \triangle CBD$

Statements	Reasons
1. D is the midpoint of $\overline{AC}$	1. Given
2. $\overline{AD} \cong \overline{CD}$	2. Definition of Midpoint
3. $\overline{AB} \cong \overline{CB}$	3. Given
4. $\overline{BD} \cong \overline{BD}$	4. Reflexive Property
5. $\triangle ABD \cong \triangle CBD$	5. SSS

In each proof the Statements are in order but the Reasons are scrambled.
Write the Reasons in the correct order.

Given: $\overline{GH}$ and $\overline{FJ}$ bisect each other.
Prove: $\triangle FGI \cong \triangle JHI$

Statements	Scrambled Reasons	Reasons
1. $\overline{GH}$ and $\overline{FJ}$ bisect each other.	1. Vertical angles are congruent.	_____
2. $\overline{GI} \cong \overline{HI}$; $\overline{FI} \cong \overline{JI}$	2. Given	_____
3. $\angle GIF \cong \angle HIJ$	3. SAS	_____
4. $\triangle FGI \cong \triangle JHI$	4. Definition of Bisect	_____

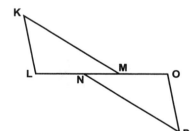

Given: KL = PO; LN = OM; KM = PN
Prove: $\triangle KLM \cong \triangle PON$

Statements	Scrambled Reasons	Reasons
1. LN = OM	1. Addition Property of Equality	_____
2. LN + NM = NM + MO	2. Given	_____
3. LN + NM = LM; NM + MO = NO	3. SSS	_____
4. LM = NO	4. Definition of Between	_____
5. KL = PO; KM = PN	5. Given	_____
6. $\triangle KLM \cong \triangle PON$	6. Substitution Property	_____

More Practice with Proofs

Complete the following proofs.
Given: m∠1 = 40°; m∠3 = 40°, ∠2 ≅ ∠4
Prove: △RTQ ≅ △TRS

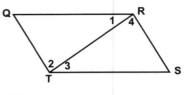

Statements	Reasons
1. m∠1 = 40°; m∠3 = 40°, ∠2 ≅ ∠4	1. _____
2. ∠1 ≅ ∠3	2. _____
3. $\overline{RT}$ ≅ $\overline{TR}$	3. _____
4. △RTQ ≅ △TRS	4. _____

Given: $\overline{WY}$ ≅ $\overline{XV}$; $\overline{VW}$ ⊥ $\overline{WX}$; $\overline{YX}$ ⊥ $\overline{WX}$
Prove: △XWV ≅ △WXY

Statements	Reasons
1. $\overline{VW}$ ⊥ $\overline{WX}$ and $\overline{YX}$ ⊥ $\overline{WX}$	1. _____
2. _____	2. Definition Perpendicular Lines
3. △XWV, △WXY are right △s	3. _____
4. _____	4. Given
5. $\overline{WX}$ ≅ $\overline{WX}$	5. _____
6. △XWV ≅ △WXY	6. _____

Given: ∠1 ≅ ∠6; ∠3 ≅ ∠4; B is the midpoint of $\overline{AC}$
Prove: △ABE ≅ △CBD

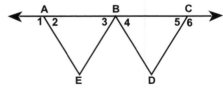

Statements	Reasons
1. _____	1. Given
2. $\overline{AB}$ ≅ $\overline{BC}$	2. _____
3. _____	3. Definition of Supplementary
4. ∠5 is supplementary to ∠6	4. _____
5. ∠2 ≅ ∠5	5. _____
6. △ABE ≅ △CBD	6. _____

Fractal: Koch Curve

> In 1975, Benoit Mandelbrot used the term **fractal** to describe natural phenomena that appear to be chaotic, fragmented, and irregular but self-similar. Fractal designs can be created by iteration. An **iteration** is a repeated operation in which the output of one step becomes the input of the next. The starting object is called the **seed.**

Example: Draw a rectangle. Perform the iteration of connecting the midpoints of the adjacent sides. Every interior rectangle looks like the original—self-similar.

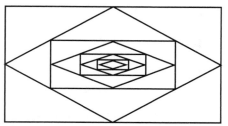

On another sheet of paper, complete Steps 0-3 to begin the Koch Curve.

Step 0   Draw a line segment 6 inches long. Consider its length to be one unit.

Ex. Step 0 _____

Step 1   Draw an equilateral triangle whose base is the middle third of the line segment. Do not draw the base.

Step 1

Step 2   Draw an equilateral triangle on each segment so the base (not drawn) of each triangle is the middle third of the corresponding segment.

Step 3   Repeat Step 2.

Complete the table.

Step	Number of Segments	Length of 1 Segment	Total Length
0	1	1	
1	4	$\frac{1}{3}$	
2			
3			

1. Describe the pattern in each column.

A. Number of segments _____

B. Length of 1 segment _____

C. Total length _____

2. What would the values be for Step 5? _____

Historical Comment: The curve is the basis for the Koch Snowflake designed by Helge von Koch in 1904. Step 0 starts with an equilateral triangle. Steps 1, 2, 3, etc., are the same.

The Coordinate Plane

Each point is designated by
two coordinates (x, y).
Point A (⁻3, 5)

The quadrants of the plane
are numbered counterclockwise
as shown.

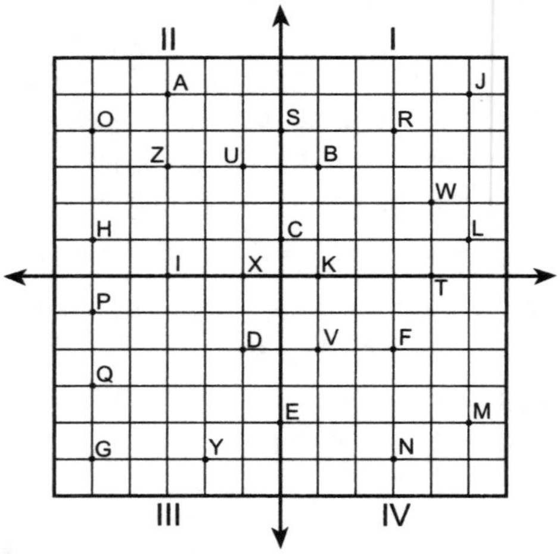

Give the coordinates of the following points.

C _____   G _____   P _____   U _____   V _____   Z _____

Use the coordinates to locate the correct letter on the graph.

1. Where is Rutherford B. Hayes buried?

___ ___ ___ ___ ___ ___ ___   ___ ___ ___ ___
(3, ⁻2) (3, 4) (0, ⁻4) (5, ⁻4) (⁻5, 4) (3, ⁻5) (4, 0)   (⁻5, 4) (⁻5, 1) (⁻3, 0) (⁻5, 4)

2. Darwin, MN claims to have the largest what?

___ ___ ___ ___   ___ ___ ___ ___ ___ ___ ___
(1, 3) (⁻3, 5) (5, 1) (5, 1)   (⁻5, 4) (3, ⁻2) (4, 0) (4, 2) (⁻3, 0) (3. ⁻5) (0, ⁻4)

3. Who was the tenth president of the United States?

___ ___ ___ ___   ___ ___ ___ ___ ___
(5, 5) (⁻5, 4) (⁻5, 1) (3, ⁻5)   (4, 0) (⁻2, ⁻5) (5, 1) (0, ⁻4) (3, 4)

4. A line is a simple figure in the coordinate plane.
   Name three points on the line.

   _____   _____   _____

5. The line passes through which quadrants?

   _____

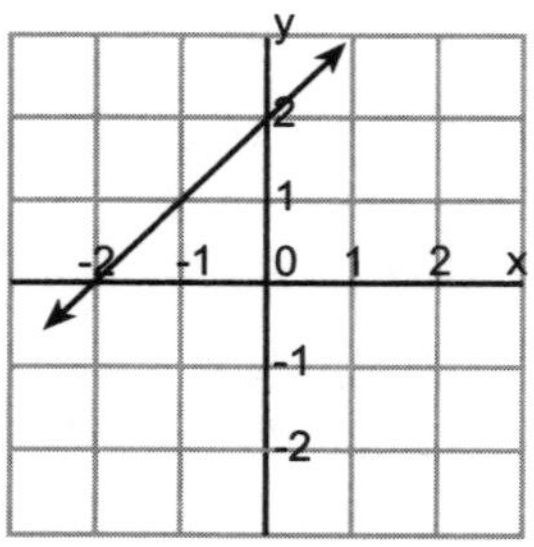

6. Give the location by quadrant(s) of the following points.
   (⁻2, ⁻5) _____   (3, ⁻1) _____

Equal x- and y-coordinates.
Opposite x- and y-coordinates.

Name _____ Date _____

Lines and Their Equations

I. Plotting Points

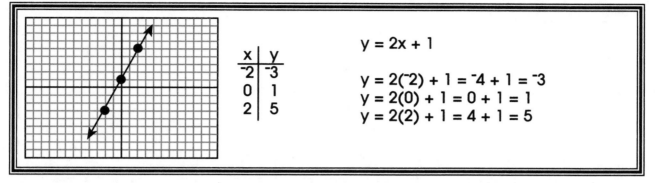

x	y
⁻2	⁻3
0	1
2	5

$y = 2x + 1$

$y = 2(⁻2) + 1 = ⁻4 + 1 = ⁻3$
$y = 2(0) + 1 = 0 + 1 = 1$
$y = 2(2) + 1 = 4 + 1 = 5$

Graph the following lines by plotting points. Use your own graph paper.

1. $y = -x + 6$

2. $y = \frac{1}{2}x - 5$

3. $2x + 3y = 6$

4. $8x - 2y = ⁻6$

5. $3x - 2y = ⁻6$

6. $x + 6 = ⁻3y$

II. Slope-Intercept

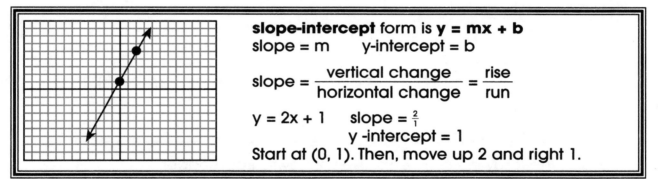

slope-intercept form is **y = mx + b**
slope = m   y-intercept = b

$$\text{slope} = \frac{\text{vertical change}}{\text{horizontal change}} = \frac{\text{rise}}{\text{run}}$$

$y = 2x + 1$ slope = $\frac{2}{1}$
            y-intercept = 1
Start at (0, 1). Then, move up 2 and right 1.

Graph the following lines by using the slope and y-intercept. Use you own graph paper.

7. $y = ⁻2x + 3$

8. $y = \frac{2}{3}x - 1$

9. $y = 4x - 3$

10. $y = \frac{1}{3}x$

11. $y = -\frac{1}{4} + 3$

12. $y = 2$

Lines and Their Equations

III. Standard Form

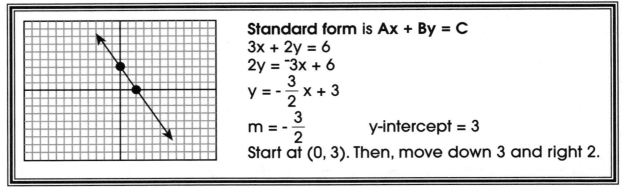

Standard form is Ax + By = C

$3x + 2y = 6$

$2y = {}^{-}3x + 6$

$y = -\dfrac{3}{2}x + 3$

$m = -\dfrac{3}{2}$ y-intercept = 3

Start at (0, 3). Then, move down 3 and right 2.

Graph the following lines by using the slope and y-intercept. Use your own graph paper.

13. $2x + 5y = 10$ 14. $3x - 4y = 12$ 15. $^{-}2x - 3y = 6$

16. $3x + 4y = 1$ 17. $^{-}2x + y = 4$ 18. $x - 3y = 2$

IV. Segments

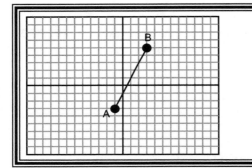

A ($^{-}$1, $^{-}$3)   B (3, 5)

and

$y = 2x - 1$ for $^{-}1 \leq x \leq 3$

are two different ways to express $\overline{AB}$.

Graph the following segments. Use your own graph paper.

19. $\overline{CD}$ C ($^{-}$2, 2) D (4, $^{-}$1)

20. $\overline{EF}$ E (0, $^{-}$4) F (5, 2)

21. $\overline{GH}$ G ($^{-}$3, $^{-}$5) H (2, 5)

22. $\overline{IJ}$ $y = \dfrac{1}{2}x + 2$ for $^{-}4 \leq x \leq 2$

23. $\overline{KL}$ $y = {}^{-}2x + 3$ for $^{-}1 \leq x \leq 3$

24. $\overline{MN}$ $2x - 3y = {}^{-}6$ for $^{-}3 \leq x3 \leq 3$

Equation of a Line in Standard Form: Ax + By = C

I. Given the slope and a point.

$$m = \frac{1}{4}, \quad (^-4, 3)$$

Use slope-intercept form and solve for b.

$y = mx + b$	$y = \frac{1}{4}x + 4$
$3 = \frac{1}{4}(^-4) + b$	$4y = x + 16$
$3 = ^-1 + b$	$-x + 4y = 16$
$4 = b$	$x - 4y = ^-16$

Match the equation of the line to the given conditions.

1. $m = ^-2, (3, 1)$ A. $3x + 2y = 5$

2. $m = 2, (1, ^-2)$ B. $2x + y = 7$

3. $m = -\frac{3}{2}, (1, 1)$ C. $x + y = 1$

4. $m = ^-1, (^-1, 2)$ D. $2x - y = 4$

5. $m = \frac{1}{3}, (6, 3)$ E. $x - 3y = ^-3$

II. Given two points

$$(1, 4), (^-1, ^-2)$$
Use slope formula to find m. Use slope-intercept form to find b.
$$m = (y_2 - y_1)/(x_2 - x_1) = (^-2 - 4)/(^-1 - 1) = ^-6/^-2 = 3$$

$y = mx + b$	$y = 3x + 1$
$4 = 3(1) + b$	$^-3x + y = 1$
$4 = 3 + b$	$3x - y = ^-1$
$1 = b$	

Match the equation of the line to the given conditions.

6. $(1, 3), (^-1, ^-1)$ F. $x + 3y = 6$

7. $(3, 1), (6, 0)$ G. $2x - 3y = ^-6$

8. $(^-3, 0), (0, 2)$ H. $2x - y = ^-1$

9. $(4, 2), (2, 4)$ I. $x + 2y = 5$

10. $(1, 2), (^-1, 3)$ J. $x + y = 6$

Equation of a Line in Standard Form: Ax + By = C

III. Given a parallel line and a point

Parallel to $y = 2x - 1$ through $(3, 5)$
Remember: Parallel lines have the same slope.

$m = 2$ $(3, 5)$

$y = mx + b$	$y = 2x - 1$
$5 = 2(3) + b$	$^-2x + y = ^-1$
$5 = 6 + b$	$2x - y = 1$
$^-1 = b$	

Match the equation of the line to the given conditions.

11. Parallel to $y = 3x + 4$ through $(0, -2)$ K. $3x + 2y = 4$
12. Parallel to $y = \frac{1}{2}x - 3$ through $(4, 2)$ L. $2x + 3y = ^-1$
13. Parallel to $2x + 3y = 6$ through $(4, -3)$ M. $3x - 4y = ^-2$
14. Parallel to $3x - 4y = 1$ through $(2, 2)$ N. $3x - y = 2$
15. Parallel to $3x + 2y = 10$ through $(1, \frac{1}{2})$ O. $x - 2y = 0$

IV. Given a perpendicular line and a point

Perpendicular to $y = 2x - 1$ through $(3, 5)$
Remember: Perpendicular lines have slopes whose product is negative one.
$y = 2x - 1$ has a slope of 2, so m will equal $-\frac{1}{2}$ because $-\frac{1}{2} \cdot 2 = -1$

$y = mx + b$	$y = -\frac{1}{2}x + \frac{13}{2}$
$5 = -\frac{1}{2}(3) + b$	$2y = -x + 13$
$5 = \frac{^-3}{2} + b$	$x + 2y = 13$
$\frac{13}{2} = b$	

Match the equation of the line to the given conditions.

16. Perpendicular to $y = 3x + 4$ through $(0, ^-2)$ P. $x + 3y = ^-6$

17. Perpendicular to $y = \frac{1}{2}x - 3$ through $(1, 4)$ Q. $2x - 3y = ^-1$

18. Perpendicular to $3x + 2y = 6$ through $(1, 1)$ R. $2x + y = 6$

19. Perpendicular to $2x - 5y = 2$ through $(2, 3)$ S. $x - y = 0$

20. Perpendicular to $x + y = 4$ through $(^-3, ^-3)$ T. $5x + 2y = 16$

V. Summary

Write the equation of the line with the following conditions.

21. $m = 4$ through $(\frac{1}{2}, ^-2)$ _____

22. Through $(2, ^-1)$ and $(8, 1)$ _____

23. Parallel to $2x - y = -3$ through $(2, ^-1)$ _____

24. Perpendicular to $3x + 6y = 5$ through $(4, 1)$ _____

Name _____   Date _____

Distance and Midpoint

Distance Formula	Midpoint Formula
$d = \sqrt{(x_2 - x_1)^2 + (y_2 - y_1)^2}$	$\left(\dfrac{x_1 + x_2}{2}, \dfrac{y_1 + y_2}{2}\right)$
$A(^-1, ^-3) \quad B(3, 5)$	$A(^-1, ^-3) \quad B(3, 5)$
$d(AB) = \sqrt{(3 - ^-1)^2 + (5 - ^-3)^2}$	$\left(\dfrac{^-1 + 3}{2}, \dfrac{^-3 + 5}{2}\right)$
$\quad = \sqrt{(4)^2 + (8)^2}$	$\left(\dfrac{2}{2}, \dfrac{2}{2}\right)$
$\quad = \sqrt{16 + 64}$	$(1, 1)$
$\quad = \sqrt{80}$	
$d(AB) = 4\sqrt{5}$	

Find the distance and the midpoint between the given points. Cross out the correct answers below. Use the remaining letters to complete the statement.

	Distance	Midpoint
1. $(^-2, 2)$ and $(4, ^-1)$	_____	_____
2. $(^-3, ^-5)$ and $(2, 5)$	_____	_____
3. $(^-1, 5)$ and $(3, ^-3)$	_____	_____
4. $(0, 0)$ and $(3, 4)$	_____	_____
5. $(1, 2)$ and $(4, 7)$	_____	_____
6. $(^-2, 4)$ and $(3, ^-5)$	_____	_____
7. $(2, 2)$ and $(6, 6)$	_____	_____
8. $(3, 6)$ and $(5, ^-2)$	_____	_____
9. $(^-1, ^-4)$ and $(3, 5)$	_____	_____

5	$(-\frac{1}{2}, 0)$	$(0, -\frac{1}{2})$	$4\sqrt{5}$	$\sqrt{5}$	10	$(1, \frac{1}{2})$	$9\sqrt{7}$	$(1, 5)$
S	Q	P	U	Y	T	M	H	G
$\sqrt{97}$	$3\sqrt{21}$	$(\frac{1}{2}, -\frac{1}{2})$	$(5/2, 9/2)$	21	$3\sqrt{5}$	$(2, 4)$	$(4, 2)$	$\sqrt{34}$
B	A	H	R	G	W	O	E	U
0	$(-1, -1)$	$5\sqrt{5}$	$2\sqrt{53}$	1	$(1\frac{1}{2}, 2)$	$(2, 1\frac{1}{2})$	$4\sqrt{17}$	$2\sqrt{17}$
R	E	S	A	N	V	T	H	S
$(1, 1)$	$(0, 0)$	34	$\sqrt{106}$	32	$4\sqrt{2}$	$(2, 2)$	$(4, 4)$	25
R	E	O	Y	R	L	E	T	M

10. This Distance Formula is based on the

_ _ _ _ _ _ _ _ _ _ _ _ _ _ _ _ _ _ _.

Angles and Parallel Lines

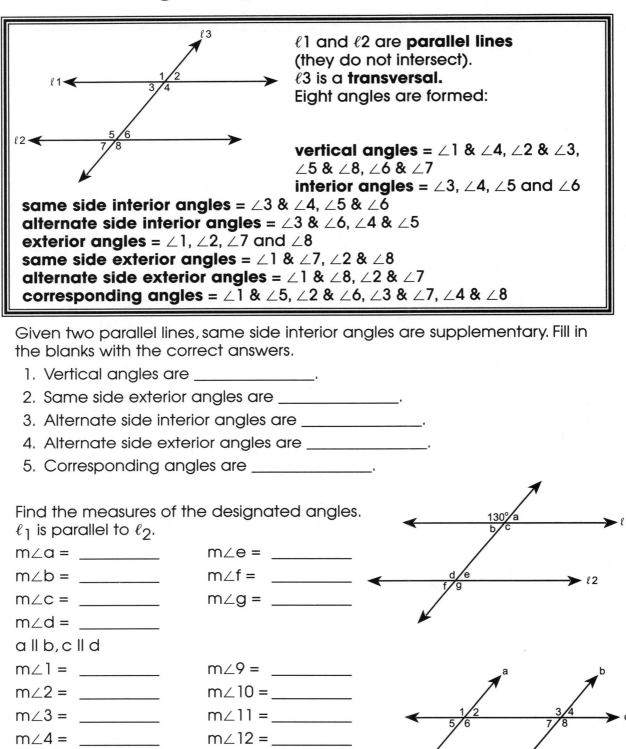

ℓ1 and ℓ2 are **parallel lines** (they do not intersect).
ℓ3 is a **transversal.**
Eight angles are formed:

vertical angles = ∠1 & ∠4, ∠2 & ∠3, ∠5 & ∠8, ∠6 & ∠7
interior angles = ∠3, ∠4, ∠5 and ∠6
same side interior angles = ∠3 & ∠4, ∠5 & ∠6
alternate side interior angles = ∠3 & ∠6, ∠4 & ∠5
exterior angles = ∠1, ∠2, ∠7 and ∠8
same side exterior angles = ∠1 & ∠7, ∠2 & ∠8
alternate side exterior angles = ∠1 & ∠8, ∠2 & ∠7
corresponding angles = ∠1 & ∠5, ∠2 & ∠6, ∠3 & ∠7, ∠4 & ∠8

Given two parallel lines, same side interior angles are supplementary. Fill in the blanks with the correct answers.

1. Vertical angles are _____.

2. Same side exterior angles are _____.

3. Alternate side interior angles are _____.

4. Alternate side exterior angles are _____.

5. Corresponding angles are _____.

Find the measures of the designated angles.
ℓ₁ is parallel to ℓ₂.

m∠a = _____   m∠e = _____
m∠b = _____   m∠f = _____
m∠c = _____   m∠g = _____
m∠d = _____

a ∥ b, c ∥ d

m∠1 = _____   m∠9 = _____
m∠2 = _____   m∠10 = _____
m∠3 = _____   m∠11 = _____
m∠4 = _____   m∠12 = _____
m∠5 = _____   m∠13 = _____
m∠6 = _____   m∠14 = _____
m∠7 = _____   m∠15 = _____
m∠8 = _____

More Angles and Parallel Lines

Find the missing values.

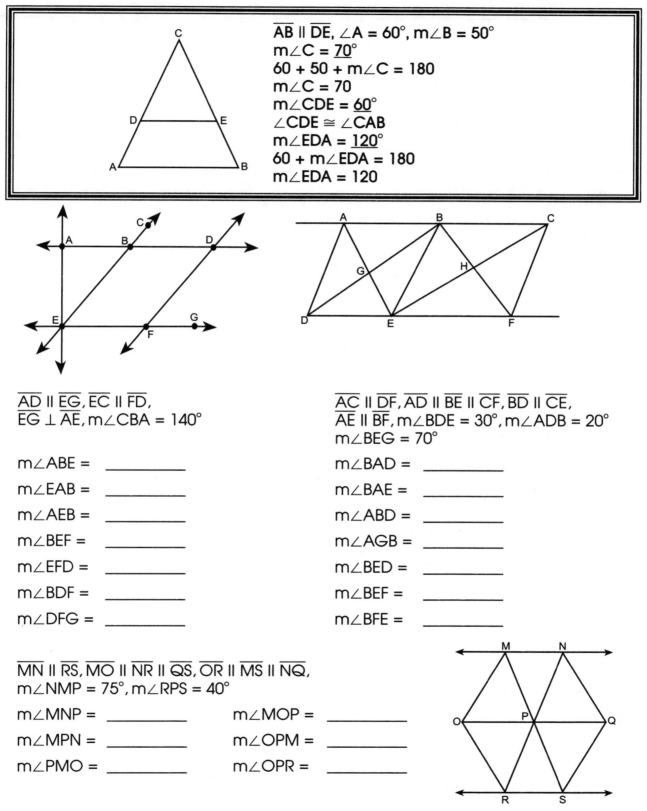

$\overline{AB} \parallel \overline{DE}$, $\angle A = 60°$, $m\angle B = 50°$
$m\angle C = \underline{70}°$
$60 + 50 + m\angle C = 180$
$m\angle C = 70$
$m\angle CDE = \underline{60}°$
$\angle CDE \cong \angle CAB$
$m\angle EDA = \underline{120}°$
$60 + m\angle EDA = 180$
$m\angle EDA = 120$

$\overline{AD} \parallel \overline{EG}$, $\overline{EC} \parallel \overline{FD}$,
$\overline{EG} \perp \overline{AE}$, $m\angle CBA = 140°$

$m\angle ABE = $ _____

$m\angle EAB = $ _____

$m\angle AEB = $ _____

$m\angle BEF = $ _____

$m\angle EFD = $ _____

$m\angle BDF = $ _____

$m\angle DFG = $ _____

$\overline{AC} \parallel \overline{DF}$, $\overline{AD} \parallel \overline{BE} \parallel \overline{CF}$, $\overline{BD} \parallel \overline{CE}$,
$\overline{AE} \parallel \overline{BF}$, $m\angle BDE = 30°$, $m\angle ADB = 20°$
$m\angle BEG = 70°$

$m\angle BAD = $ _____

$m\angle BAE = $ _____

$m\angle ABD = $ _____

$m\angle AGB = $ _____

$m\angle BED = $ _____

$m\angle BEF = $ _____

$m\angle BFE = $ _____

$\overline{MN} \parallel \overline{RS}$, $\overline{MO} \parallel \overline{NR} \parallel \overline{QS}$, $\overline{OR} \parallel \overline{MS} \parallel \overline{NQ}$,
$m\angle NMP = 75°$, $m\angle RPS = 40°$

$m\angle MNP = $ _____ $m\angle MOP = $ _____

$m\angle MPN = $ _____ $m\angle OPM = $ _____

$m\angle PMO = $ _____ $m\angle OPR = $ _____

Proofs Using Parallel Lines

Complete the following proofs.

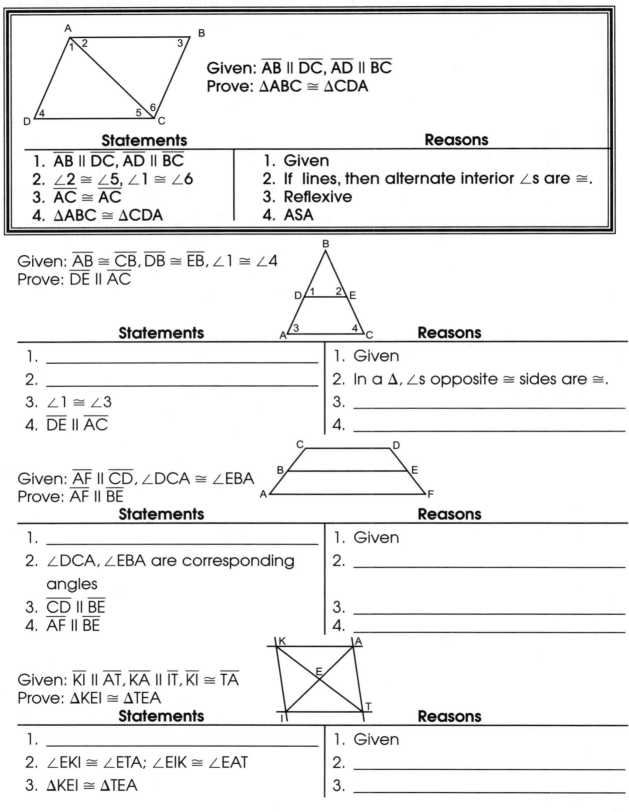

Given: $\overline{AB} \parallel \overline{DC}$, $\overline{AD} \parallel \overline{BC}$
Prove: $\triangle ABC \cong \triangle CDA$

Statements	Reasons
1. $\overline{AB} \parallel \overline{DC}$, $\overline{AD} \parallel \overline{BC}$	1. Given
2. $\angle 2 \cong \angle 5$, $\angle 1 \cong \angle 6$	2. If lines, then alternate interior $\angle$s are $\cong$.
3. $\overline{AC} \cong \overline{AC}$	3. Reflexive
4. $\triangle ABC \cong \triangle CDA$	4. ASA

Given: $\overline{AB} \cong \overline{CB}$, $\overline{DB} \cong \overline{EB}$, $\angle 1 \cong \angle 4$
Prove: $\overline{DE} \parallel \overline{AC}$

Statements	Reasons
1. _____	1. Given
2. _____	2. In a $\triangle$, $\angle$s opposite $\cong$ sides are $\cong$.
3. $\angle 1 \cong \angle 3$	3. _____
4. $\overline{DE} \parallel \overline{AC}$	4. _____

Given: $\overline{AF} \parallel \overline{CD}$, $\angle DCA \cong \angle EBA$
Prove: $\overline{AF} \parallel \overline{BE}$

Statements	Reasons
1. _____	1. Given
2. $\angle DCA$, $\angle EBA$ are corresponding angles	2. _____
3. $\overline{CD} \parallel \overline{BE}$	3. _____
4. $\overline{AF} \parallel \overline{BE}$	4. _____

Given: $\overline{KI} \parallel \overline{AT}$, $\overline{KA} \parallel \overline{IT}$, $\overline{KI} \cong \overline{TA}$
Prove: $\triangle KEI \cong \triangle TEA$

Statements	Reasons
1. _____	1. Given
2. $\angle EKI \cong \angle ETA$; $\angle EIK \cong \angle EAT$	2. _____
3. $\triangle KEI \cong \triangle TEA$	3. _____

More Proofs

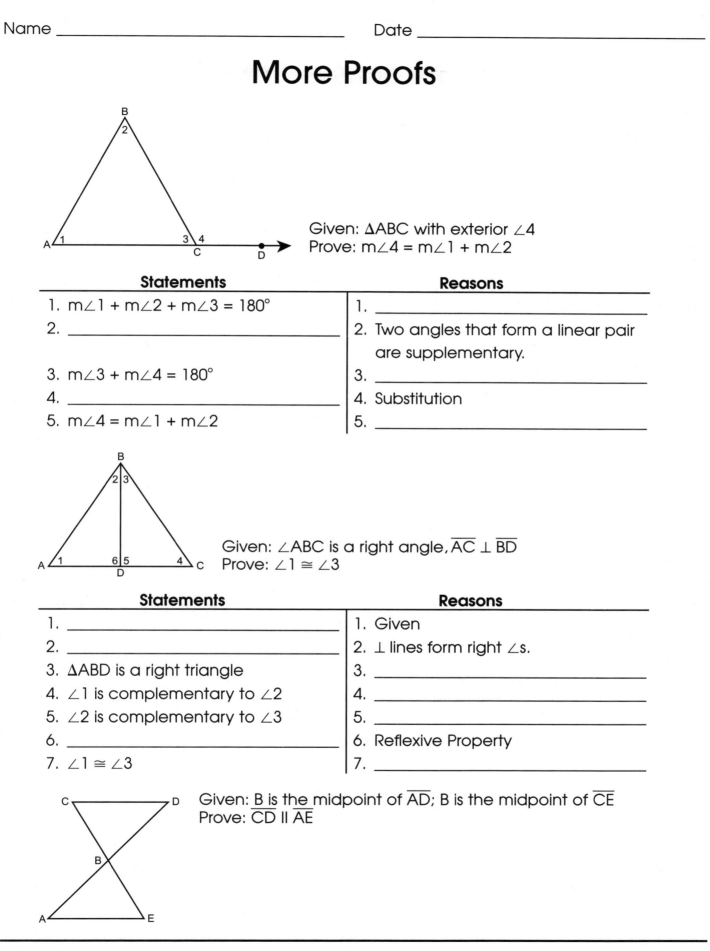

Given: △ABC with exterior ∠4
Prove: m∠4 = m∠1 + m∠2

Statements	Reasons
1. m∠1 + m∠2 + m∠3 = 180°	1. _____
2. _____	2. Two angles that form a linear pair are supplementary.
3. m∠3 + m∠4 = 180°	3. _____
4. _____	4. Substitution
5. m∠4 = m∠1 + m∠2	5. _____

Given: ∠ABC is a right angle, $\overline{AC} \perp \overline{BD}$
Prove: ∠1 ≅ ∠3

Statements	Reasons
1. _____	1. Given
2. _____	2. ⊥ lines form right ∠s.
3. △ABD is a right triangle	3. _____
4. ∠1 is complementary to ∠2	4. _____
5. ∠2 is complementary to ∠3	5. _____
6. _____	6. Reflexive Property
7. ∠1 ≅ ∠3	7. _____

Given: B is the midpoint of $\overline{AD}$; B is the midpoint of $\overline{CE}$
Prove: $\overline{CD} \parallel \overline{AE}$

Railroad Tracks or Intersections

State three solutions for each equation.
Graph each equation.

1. $y = 3x - 4$ (,)   (,)   (,)

2. $y = 3x - 1$ (,)   (,)   (,)

3. $y = x - 4$ (,)   (,)   (,)

4. Compare the graphs for equations 1 and 2.

_____

5. What do equations 1 and 2 have in common?

_____

6. Compare the graphs for equations 1 and 3.

_____

7. What do equations 1 and 3 have in common?

_____

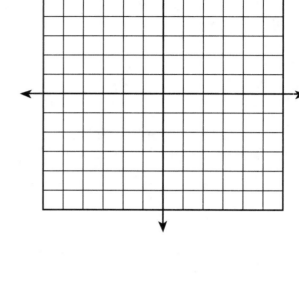

State three solutions for each equation.
Graph each equation.

8. $y = (\frac{2}{3})x + 3$ (,)   (,)   (,)

9. $y = (-\frac{3}{2})x + 1$ (,)   (,)   (,)

10. $y = 2x + 1$ (,)   (,)   (,)

11. Compare the graphs for equations 8 and 9.

_____

12. Compare equations for 8 and 9.

_____

13. Compare the graphs for equations 9 and 10.

_____

14. What do equations 9 and 10 have in common?

_____

15. *Parallel lines* never intersect. Graphs of equations ____ and ____ are parallel.
Perpendicular lines intersect forming right angles. Graphs of equations ____ and
____ are perpendicular.

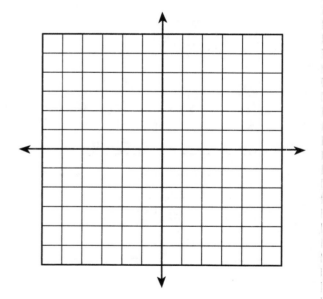

Fun with Graphing

Draw the segments with the following endpoints on the graphs on page 44.

I. What does this figure look like? _____

1. (15, 0), (0, 1)	11. (5, 0), (0, 11)	21. (⁻10, 0), (0, ⁻6)
2. (14, 0), (0, 2)	12. (4, 0), (0, 12)	22. (⁻9, 0), (0, ⁻7)
3. (13, 0), (0, 3)	13. (3, 0), (0, 13)	23. (⁻8, 0), (0, ⁻8)
4. (12, 0), (0, 4)	14. (2, 0), (0, 14)	24. (⁻7, 0), (0, ⁻9)
5. (11, 0), (0, 5)	15. (1, 0), (0, 15)	25. (⁻6, 0), (0, ⁻10)
6. (10, 0), (0, 6)	16. (⁻15, 0), (0, ⁻1)	26. (⁻5, 0), (0, ⁻11)
7. (9, 0), (0, 7)	17. (⁻14, 0), (0, ⁻2)	27. (4, 0), (0, ⁻12)
8. (8, 0), (0, 8)	18. (⁻13, 0), (0, ⁻3)	28. (⁻3, 0), (0, ⁻13)
9. (7, 0), (0, 9)	19. (⁻12, 0), (0, ⁻4)	29. (⁻2, 0), (0, ⁻14)
10. (6, 0), (0, 10)	20. (⁻11, 0), (0, ⁻5)	30. (⁻1, 0), (0, ⁻15)

II. What does this figure look like? _____

1. (12, 12), (12, ⁻12)	19. (⁻12, 8), (⁻7, ⁻12)	37. (4, ⁻12), (12, 5)
2. (12, ⁻12), (⁻12, ⁻12)	20. (⁻12, 6), (⁻5, ⁻12)	38. (6, ⁻12), (12, 7)
3. (⁻12, ⁻12), (⁻12, 12)	21. (⁻12, 4), (⁻3, ⁻12)	39. (8, ⁻12), (12, 9)
4. (⁻12, 12), (12, 12)	22. (⁻12, 2), (⁻1, ⁻12)	40. (10, ⁻12), (12, 11)
5. (12, 12), (⁻12, 11)	23. (⁻12, 0), (1, ⁻12)	41. (12, ⁻12), (11, 12)
6. (10, 12), (⁻12, 9)	24. (⁻12, ⁻2), (3, ⁻12)	42. (12, ⁻10), (9, 12)
7. (8, 12), (⁻12, 7)	25. (⁻12, ⁻4), (5, ⁻12)	43. (12, ⁻8), (7, 12)
8. (6, 12), (⁻12, 5)	26. (⁻12, ⁻6), (7, ⁻12)	44. (12, ⁻6), (5, 12)
9. (4, 12), (⁻12, 3)	27. (⁻12, ⁻8), (9, ⁻12)	45. (12, ⁻4), (3, 12)
10. (2, 12), (⁻12, 1)	28. (⁻12, ⁻10), (11, ⁻12)	46. (12, ⁻2), (1, 12)
11. (0, 12), (⁻12, ⁻1)	29. (⁻12, ⁻12), (12, ⁻11)	47. (12, 0), (⁻1, 12)
12. (⁻2, 12), (⁻12, ⁻3)	30. (⁻10, ⁻12), (12, ⁻9)	48. (12, 2), (⁻3, 12)
13. (⁻4, 12), (⁻12, -5)	31. (⁻8, ⁻12), (12, ⁻7)	49. (12, 4) (⁻5, 12)
14. (⁻6, 12), (⁻12, ⁻7)	32. (⁻6, ⁻12), (12, ⁻5)	50. (12, 6), (⁻7, 12)
15. (⁻8, 12), (⁻12, ⁻9)	33. (⁻4, ⁻12), (12, ⁻3)	51. (12, 8), (⁻9, 12)
16. (⁻10, 12), (⁻12, ⁻11)	34. (⁻2, ⁻12), (12, ⁻1)	52. (12, 10), (⁻11, 12)
17. (-12, 12), (-11, -12)	35. (0, -12), (12, 1)	
18. (⁻12, 10), (⁻9, ⁻12)	36. (2, ⁻12), (12, 3)	

© McGraw-Hill Children's Publishing

0-7424-1776-X *Geometry*

Fun with Graphing

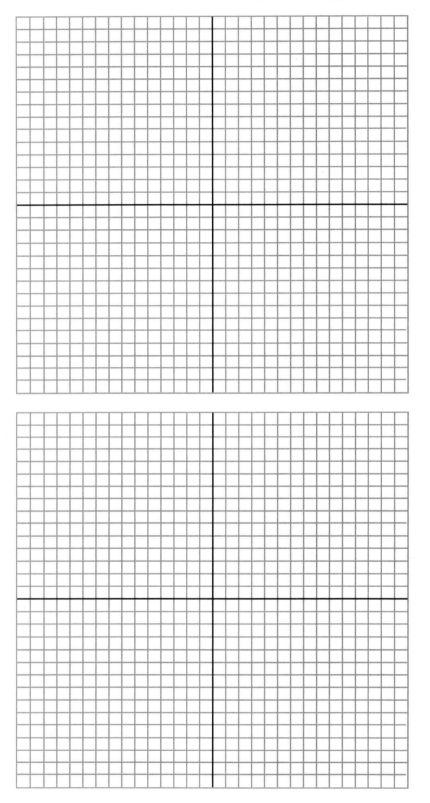

Constructing Congruent Segments

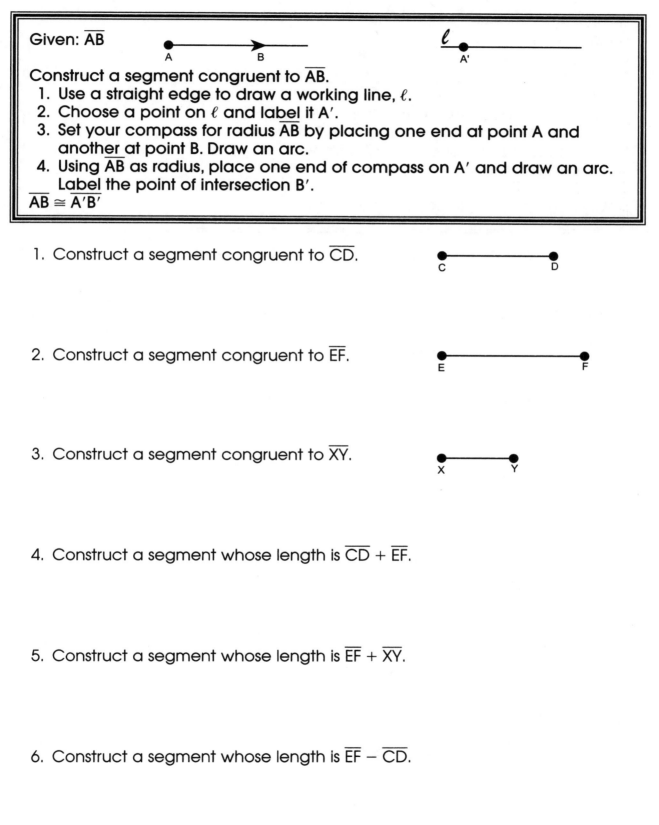

Given: $\overline{AB}$

A •———————→— B

ℓ •———————————— A'

Construct a segment congruent to $\overline{AB}$.
1. Use a straight edge to draw a working line, ℓ.
2. Choose a point on ℓ and label it A'.
3. Set your compass for radius $\overline{AB}$ by placing one end at point A and another at point B. Draw an arc.
4. Using $\overline{AB}$ as radius, place one end of compass on A' and draw an arc. Label the point of intersection B'.
$\overline{AB} \cong \overline{A'B'}$

1. Construct a segment congruent to $\overline{CD}$.

C •————————————• D

2. Construct a segment congruent to $\overline{EF}$.

E •————————————————• F

3. Construct a segment congruent to $\overline{XY}$.

X •————————• Y

4. Construct a segment whose length is $\overline{CD} + \overline{EF}$.

5. Construct a segment whose length is $\overline{EF} + \overline{XY}$.

6. Construct a segment whose length is $\overline{EF} - \overline{CD}$.

Constructing Perpendicular Bisectors

Given: $\overline{AB}$

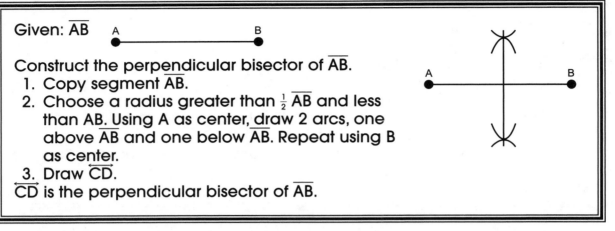

Construct the perpendicular bisector of $\overline{AB}$.
  1. Copy segment $\overline{AB}$.
  2. Choose a radius greater than $\frac{1}{2}$ $\overline{AB}$ and less than AB. Using A as center, draw 2 arcs, one above $\overline{AB}$ and one below $\overline{AB}$. Repeat using B as center.
  3. Draw $\overleftrightarrow{CD}$.
$\overleftrightarrow{CD}$ is the perpendicular bisector of $\overline{AB}$.

I. Construct the perpendicular bisector of the following.

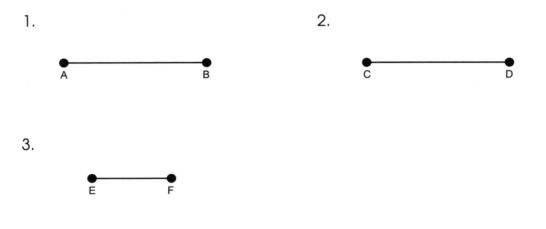

1.

A ———————— B

2.

C ———————— D

3.

E ——— F

II. Bisect side $\overline{YZ}$ of $\triangle XYZ$.

4.

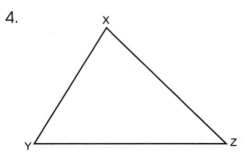

5. Construct a segment whose length equals $\overline{XY} + \overline{YZ} + \overline{XZ}$.

Constructing Perpendiculars, Given a Point on the Line

Given: Point A on line ℓ

Construct the perpendicular to point A.
1. Copy ℓ.
2. Using A as center choose any radius, less than ℓ. Draw arcs intersecting ℓ. Label them C and D.
3. Using C as center, choose a radius greater than CA. Draw an arc above ℓ. Repeat using D as center with same radius.
4. Draw $\overleftrightarrow{XA}$.
$\overleftrightarrow{XA}$ is perpendicular to ℓ at point A.

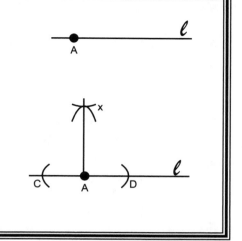

I. Construct perpendicular lines to the given points.

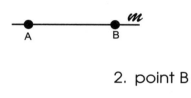

1. point A

2. point B

3. point C

4. point D

Constructing Perpendiculars, Given a Point NOT on the Line

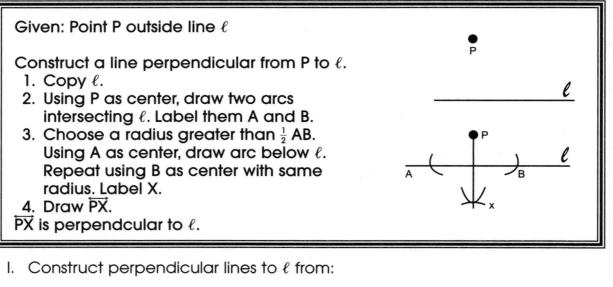

Given: Point P outside line ℓ

Construct a line perpendicular from P to ℓ.
  1. Copy ℓ.
  2. Using P as center, draw two arcs intersecting ℓ. Label them A and B.
  3. Choose a radius greater than $\frac{1}{2}$ AB. Using A as center, draw arc below ℓ. Repeat using B as center with same radius. Label X.
  4. Draw $\overleftrightarrow{PX}$.
$\overleftrightarrow{PX}$ is perpendcular to ℓ.

I. Construct perpendicular lines to ℓ from:

  1. point A

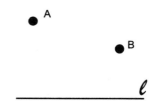

  2. point B

II. Construct the perpendicular lines from each vertex to the opposite side in $\triangle ABC$.

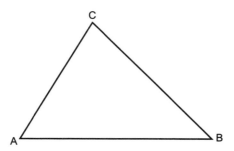

Constructing Congruent Angles

Given: ∠XYZ

Construct an angle congruent to ∠XYZ.
1. Draw a ray, label it Y'Z'.
2. Using Y as center, choose any radius and draw an arc that intersects $\overrightarrow{YX}$ and $\overrightarrow{YZ}$. Label points S and T.
3. Using Y' as center and the same radius, draw an arc intersecting $\overrightarrow{Y'Z'}$. Label the point of intersection Q.
4. Using T as center, find radius equal to TS. Draw arc through point S.
5. Using Q as center, draw arc using radius equal to TS. Label point of intersection P.
6. Draw $\overrightarrow{Y'P}$.
∠XYZ ≅ ∠PY'Z'.

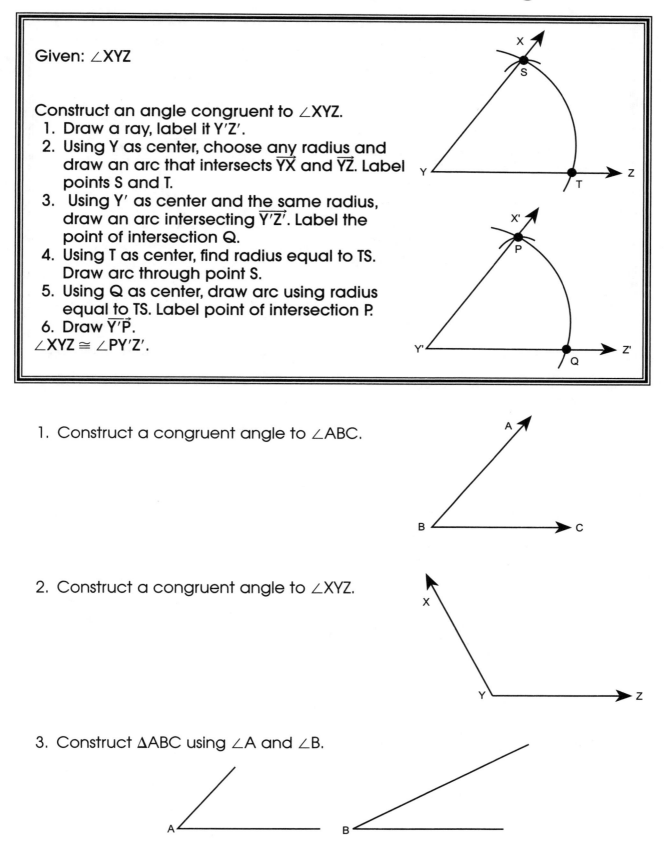

1. Construct a congruent angle to ∠ABC.

2. Construct a congruent angle to ∠XYZ.

3. Construct △ABC using ∠A and ∠B.

Constructing Angle Bisectors

Given: ∠ABC

Construct an angle bisector.
1. Copy ∠ABC.
2. Using B′ as center, choose any radius, and draw an arc intersecting $\overrightarrow{B'A'}$ and $\overrightarrow{B'C'}$.
3. Using X as center, choose a radius greater than $\frac{1}{2}$ XY, draw an arc in the interior of ∠A′B′C′. Repeat using Y as center and same radius. Label point of intersection Z.
4. Draw $\overrightarrow{B'Z'}$.
$\overrightarrow{B'Z}$ bisects ∠A′B′C′.

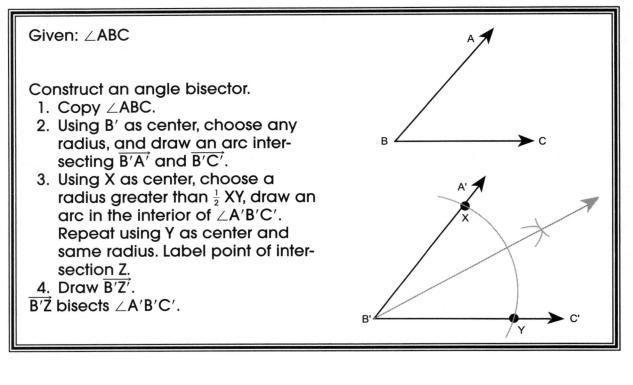

1. Bisect ∠XYZ.

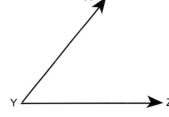

2. Bisect ∠ABC.

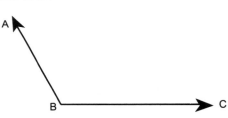

3. Construct a 45° angle.
   (Hint: Construct perpendicular lines first.)

4. Construct an equilateral Δ. Use AB as the length of each side.

5. What is the measurement of each angle in #4? _____

6. Construct a 30° angle.
   (Hint: Use your equilateral Δ.)

         0-7424-1776-X *Geometry*

Constructing Parallel Lines

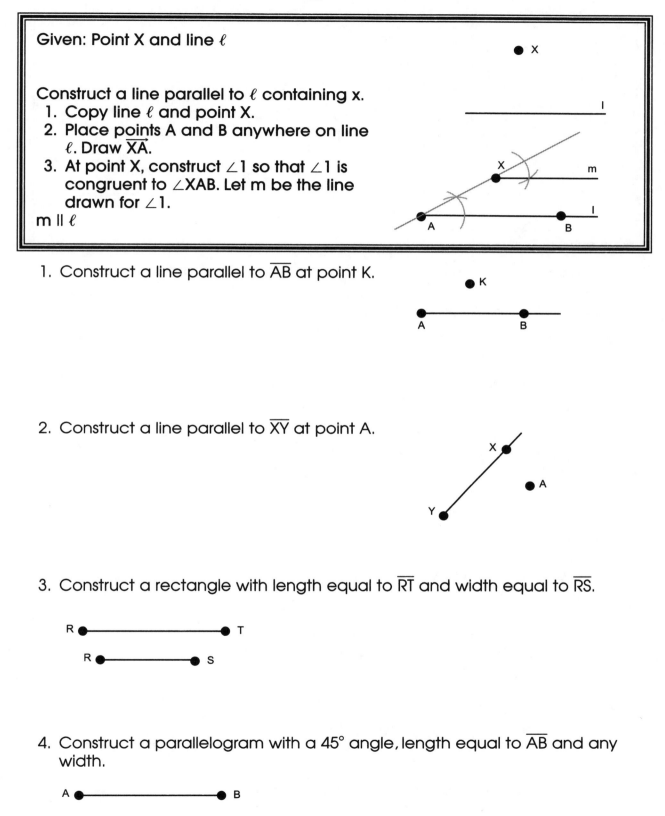

Given: Point X and line ℓ

Construct a line parallel to ℓ containing x.
1. Copy line ℓ and point X.
2. Place points A and B anywhere on line ℓ. Draw $\overrightarrow{XA}$.
3. At point X, construct ∠1 so that ∠1 is congruent to ∠XAB. Let m be the line drawn for ∠1.

m ‖ ℓ

1. Construct a line parallel to $\overline{AB}$ at point K.

2. Construct a line parallel to $\overline{XY}$ at point A.

3. Construct a rectangle with length equal to $\overline{RT}$ and width equal to $\overline{RS}$.

4. Construct a parallelogram with a 45° angle, length equal to $\overline{AB}$ and any width.

Nonlinear Equations—Parabolas

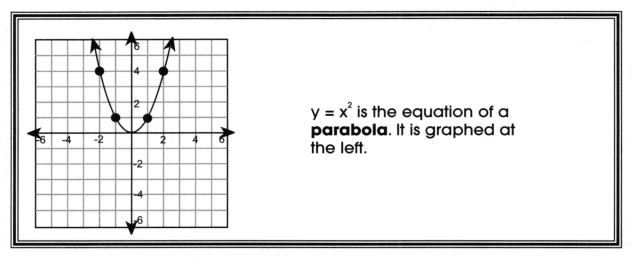

$y = x^2$ is the equation of a **parabola**. It is graphed at the left.

1. Looking at the curve $y = x^2$, what do you think the graph of $y = 2x^2$ would look like? _____
   Sketch the graph of $y = 2x^2$.

2. Sketch the graph of $y = \dfrac{1}{2} x^2$.

3. Sketch the graph of $y = x^2 + 2$.

4. Sketch the graph of $y = (x + 2)^2$.

5. Sketch the graph of $y = -x^2$.

6. What do you expect $y = (x - 3)^2 + 1$ to look like? _____
   Check your answer by graphing the equation.

7. What do you expect $y = (x + 1)^2 - 2$ to look like? _____
   Check your answer by graphing the equation.

8. What do you expect $y = 3x^2 - 2$ to look like? _____
   Check your answer by graphing the equation.

Nonlinear Equations—Circles

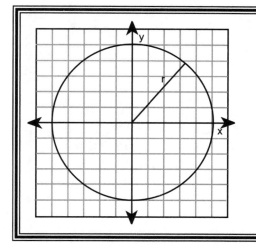

The graph of $x^2 + y^2 = r^2$ is a **circle** with radius r and center at the origin. A more general equation can be derived from the distance formula.

$$\sqrt{(x - a)^2 + (y - b)^2} = r \rightarrow (x - a)^2 + (y - b)^2 = r^2$$

This is an equation for a circle with radius r and center at (a, b).

1. Graph the following equations by plotting points.
   a. $x^2 + y^2 = 4$
   b. $x^2 + y^2 = 25$
   c. $(x - 1)^2 + (y + 1)^2 = 16$
   d. $(x + 2)^2 + (y - 2)^2 = 9$

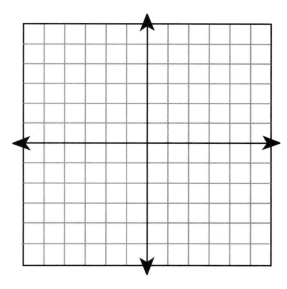
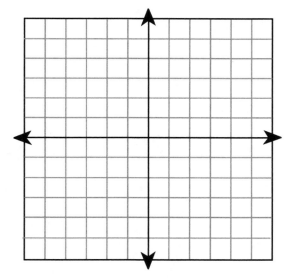

2. Give the center and radius for the circles below.
   a. $x^2 + y^2 = 9$
   b. $(x - 3)^2 + (y - 4)^2 = 16$
   c. $(x + 2)^2 + (y - 1)^2 = 4$
   d. $x^2 + (y + 3)^2 = 25$
   e. $(x - 1)^2 + (y + 2)^2 = 4$
   f. $(x + 5)^2 + (y - 3)^2 = 81$
   g. $(x - 7)^2 + (y + 5)^2 = 24$
   h. $(x - 3)^2 + (y - 3)^2 = 18$

3. Write the equations of the following circles.
   a. r = 1   (2, ⁻3)
   b. r = 2   (3, 4)
   c. r = 3   (2, 2)
   d. r = 6   (0, 0)
   e. r = 5   (⁻1, ⁻3)
   f. r = 2   (⁻2, 4)
   g. r = 1   (3, ⁻2)
   h. r = 4   (⁻2, ⁻3)

Nonlinear Equations—Ellipses

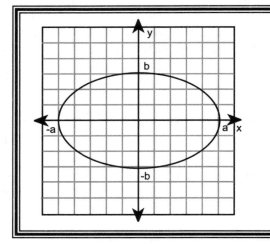

The standard form for the equation of an **ellipse** is

$$\frac{x^2}{a^2} + \frac{y^2}{b^2} = 1$$

This gives an ellipse with its center at the origin and its major axis along the x-axis with a length of 2a and its minor axis along the y-axis with a length of 2b. (a > b)

1. Graph the following equations.

   a. $\dfrac{x^2}{9} + \dfrac{y^2}{4} = 1$

   b. $\dfrac{x^2}{25} + \dfrac{y^2}{16} = 1$

   *c. $\dfrac{3x^2}{2} + \dfrac{3y^2}{1} = 6$

   *d. $4x^2 + 9y^2 = 36$

   (*Hint: Put these in standard form before graphing.)

2. The following are not in standard form.
   Identify major and minor axes and graph them.

   a. $4x^2 + y^2 = 16$

   b. $\dfrac{5x^2}{4} + \dfrac{4y^2}{5} = 20$

   *c. $\dfrac{(x-3)^2}{25} + \dfrac{(y-4)^2}{16} = 1$

   *d. $4(x + 2)^2 + 9y^2 = 36$

   (Hint: You've seen something similar to this with circles.)

3. Write the equation for an ellipse with the following perimeters.
   a. a = 3, b = 2, center (0, 0)
   b. a = 4, b = 3, center (1, 2)
   c. a = 6, b = 3, center (⁻3, 4)
   d. a = 12, b = 5, center (⁻2, ⁻4)

Name _____   Date _____

Nonlinear Equations—Hyperbola

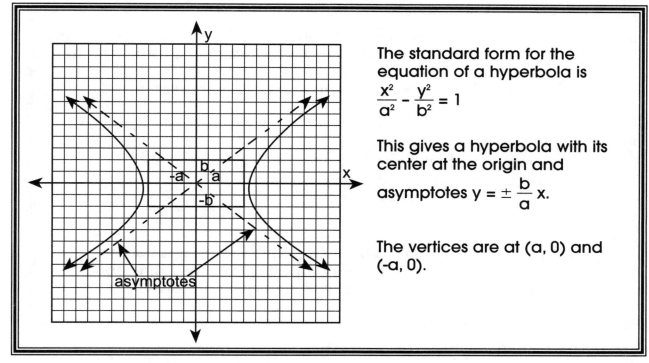

The standard form for the equation of a hyperbola is

$$\frac{x^2}{a^2} - \frac{y^2}{b^2} = 1$$

This gives a hyperbola with its center at the origin and asymptotes $y = \pm \dfrac{b}{a} x$.

The vertices are at $(a, 0)$ and $(-a, 0)$.

1. Graph the following equations.

   a. $\dfrac{x^2}{9} - \dfrac{y^2}{4} = 1$ c. $\dfrac{y^2}{9} - \dfrac{x^2}{4} = 1$

   b. $\dfrac{x^2}{4} - \dfrac{y^2}{9} = 1$ d. $\dfrac{y^2}{4} - \dfrac{x^2}{9} = 1$

2. The following are not in standard form. Identify asymptotes and graph them.

   a. $x^2 - 4y^2 = 4$ c. $(x + 1)^2 - 9(y - 1)^2 = 9$

   b. $4x^2 - 9y^2 = 36$ d. $(x - 1)^2 - (y - 2)^2 = 4$

3. Write the equation for a hyperbola with the following perimeters.*

   a. $a = 2, b = 4,$ center $(2, ^-1)$

   b. $a = 3, b = 5,$ center $(3, 2)$

   c. $a = 1, b = 3,$ center $(^-2, 4)$

   d. $a = 4, b = 2,$ center $(^-1, ^-3)$

   (*All open in the x direction.)

Ways to Prove Triangles Similar

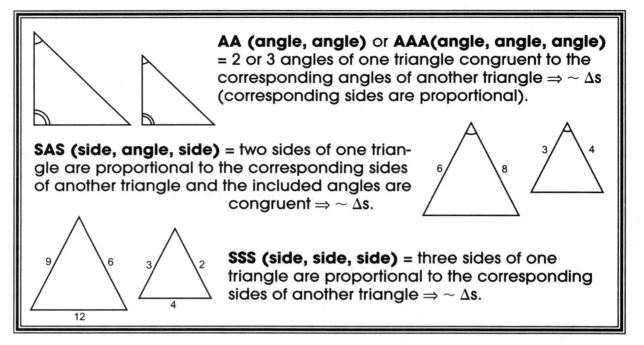

AA (angle, angle) or **AAA(angle, angle, angle)** = 2 or 3 angles of one triangle congruent to the corresponding angles of another triangle ⇒ ~ Δs (corresponding sides are proportional).

SAS (side, angle, side) = two sides of one triangle are proportional to the corresponding sides of another triangle and the included angles are congruent ⇒ ~ Δs.

SSS (side, side, side) = three sides of one triangle are proportional to the corresponding sides of another triangle ⇒ ~ Δs.

Identify which property will prove these triangles similar.

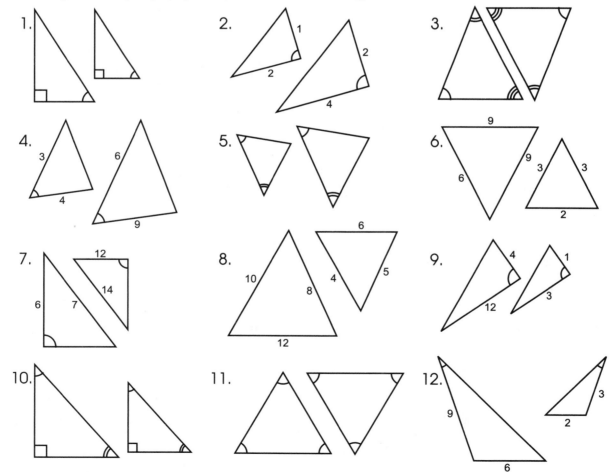

Working with Similar Triangles

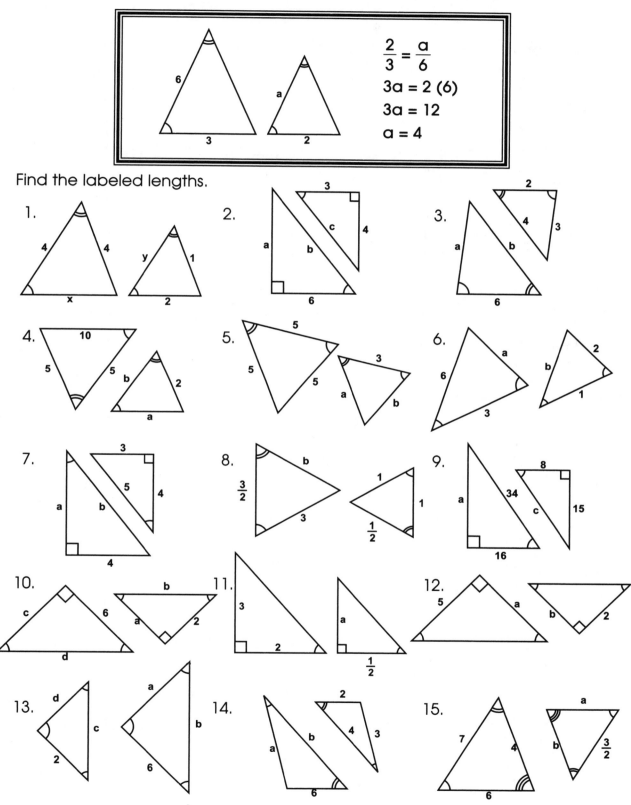

Find the labeled lengths.

More Similar Triangles

Find the area of the following triangles. (Hint: A = $\frac{1}{2}$ bh)

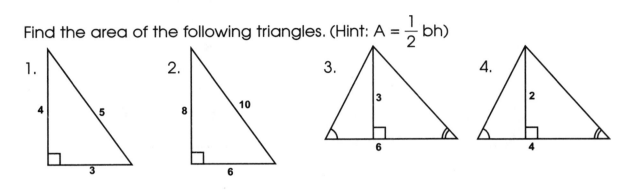

1.

2.

3.

4.

5. What is the ratio of the sides in #1 and #2? _____
6. What is the ratio of the sides in #3 and #4? _____
7. What is the ratio of the areas in #1 and #2? _____
8. What is the ratio of the areas in #3 and #4? _____
9. What can you conclude about this? _____

Find the ratio of the areas in the following sets of similar triangles with corresponding sides labeled.

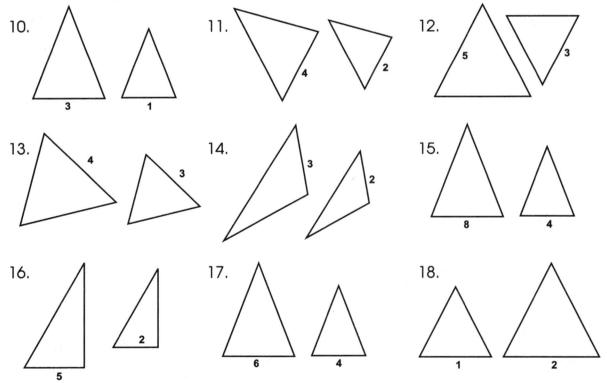

10.

11.

12.

13.

14.

15.

16.

17.

18.

Two-Column Proofs

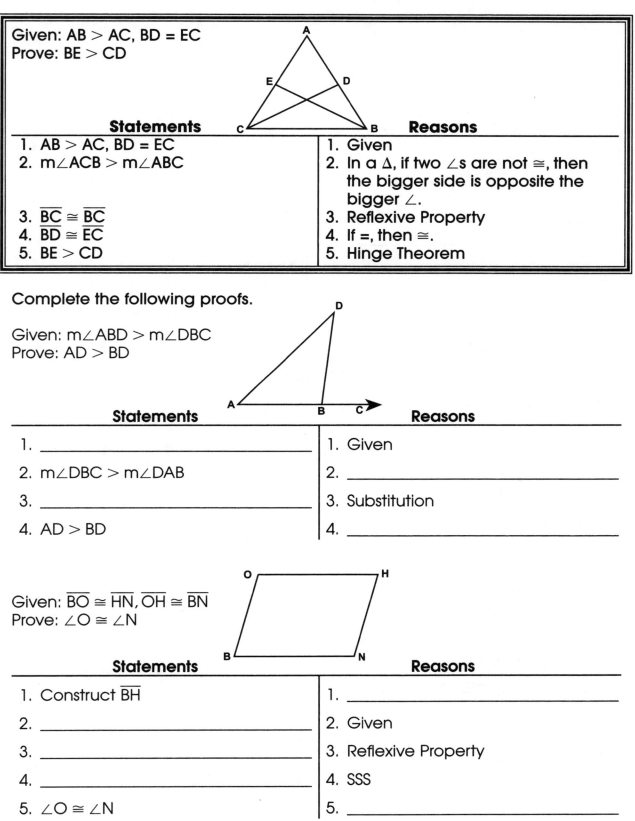

Given: AB > AC, BD = EC
Prove: BE > CD

Statements	Reasons
1. AB > AC, BD = EC	1. Given
2. m∠ACB > m∠ABC	2. In a Δ, if two ∠s are not ≅, then the bigger side is opposite the bigger ∠.
3. $\overline{BC} \cong \overline{BC}$	3. Reflexive Property
4. $\overline{BD} \cong \overline{EC}$	4. If =, then ≅.
5. BE > CD	5. Hinge Theorem

Complete the following proofs.

Given: m∠ABD > m∠DBC
Prove: AD > BD

Statements	Reasons
1. _____	1. Given
2. m∠DBC > m∠DAB	2. _____
3. _____	3. Substitution
4. AD > BD	4. _____

Given: $\overline{BO} \cong \overline{HN}, \overline{OH} \cong \overline{BN}$
Prove: ∠O ≅ ∠N

Statements	Reasons
1. Construct $\overline{BH}$	1. _____
2. _____	2. Given
3. _____	3. Reflexive Property
4. _____	4. SSS
5. ∠O ≅ ∠N	5. _____

More Two-Column Proofs

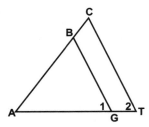

Given: $\overline{CT} \parallel \overline{BG}$
Prove: $\triangle CAT \sim \triangle BAG$

Statements	Reasons
1. _____	1. Given
2. _____	2. If ∥ lines, then corresponding ∠s are ≅ .
3. _____	3. Reflexive Property
4. $\triangle CAT \sim \triangle BAG$	4. _____

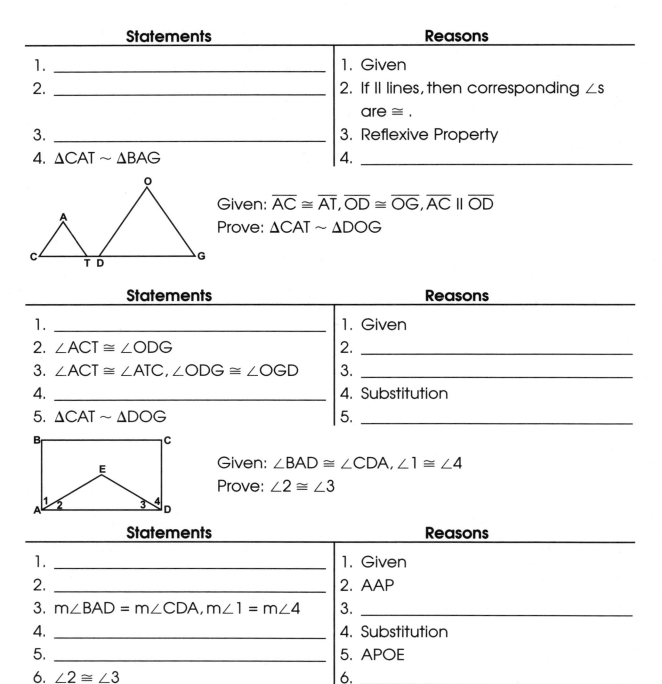

Given: $\overline{AC} \cong \overline{AT}, \overline{OD} \cong \overline{OG}, \overline{AC} \parallel \overline{OD}$
Prove: $\triangle CAT \sim \triangle DOG$

Statements	Reasons
1. _____	1. Given
2. ∠ACT ≅ ∠ODG	2. _____
3. ∠ACT ≅ ∠ATC, ∠ODG ≅ ∠OGD	3. _____
4. _____	4. Substitution
5. $\triangle CAT \sim \triangle DOG$	5. _____

Given: ∠BAD ≅ ∠CDA, ∠1 ≅ ∠4
Prove: ∠2 ≅ ∠3

Statements	Reasons
1. _____	1. Given
2. _____	2. AAP
3. m∠BAD = m∠CDA, m∠1 = m∠4	3. _____
4. _____	4. Substitution
5. _____	5. APOE
6. ∠2 ≅ ∠3	6. _____

Right Triangles

The area of a right triangle is half the product of the legs.

$$A = \frac{1}{2}(3)(4)$$

$$A = 6 \text{ Square units}$$

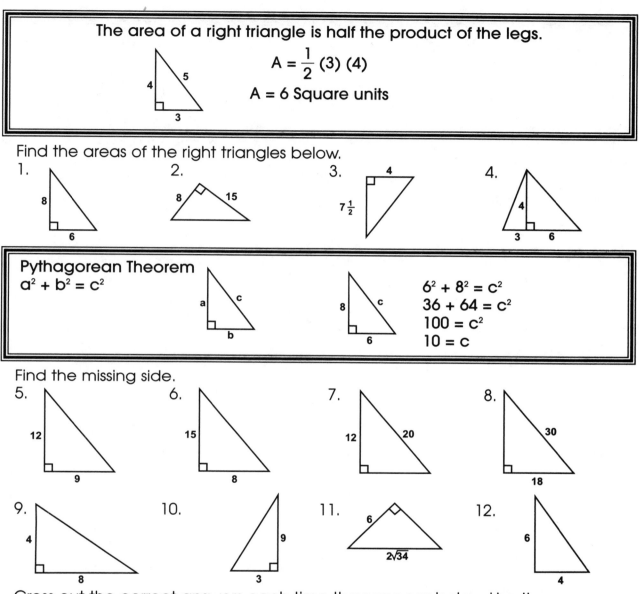

Find the areas of the right triangles below.

1.   2.   3.   4.

Pythagorean Theorem
$$a^2 + b^2 = c^2$$

$$6^2 + 8^2 = c^2$$
$$36 + 64 = c^2$$
$$100 = c^2$$
$$10 = c$$

Find the missing side.

5.   6.   7.   8.

9.   10.   11.   12.

Cross out the correct answers each time they appear below. Use the remaining letters to complete the statement.

28	16	15	$10\sqrt{3}$	$3\sqrt{10}$	90	8	16	6	24
P	S	Q	Y	U	T	H	E	A	R
17	5	$4\sqrt{5}$	20	26	$2\sqrt{13}$	36	9	10	45
E	G	I	O	R	M	E	A	O	N
49	7	15	4	120	10	6	16	23	$2\sqrt{15}$
T	R	T	I	P	E	L	R	E	S

Sets of numbers like 3, 4, 5 and 5, 12, 13 are called

_ _ _ _ _ _ _ _ _ _ _ _ _   _ _ _ _ _ _ _.

Why is this term appropriate? _____

Special Right Triangles

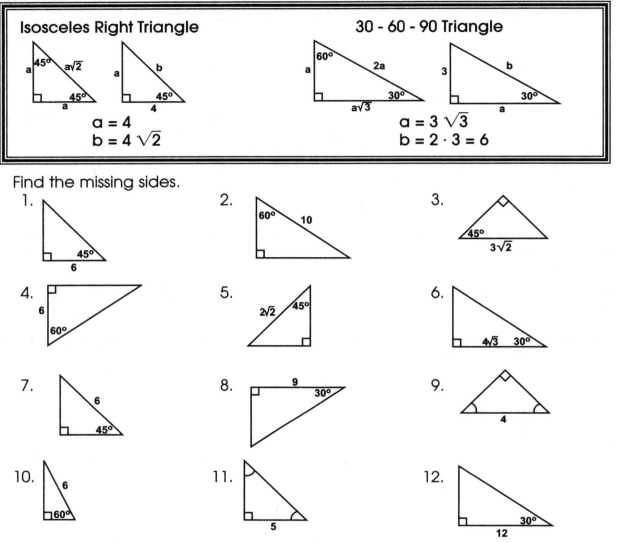

Find the missing sides.

Cross out the correct answers. The remaining letters (one per space) complete the statement.

5	9	$6\sqrt{2}$	3	10	$3\sqrt{2}$	3	$4\sqrt{3}$	$3\sqrt{2}$	12	$2\sqrt{2}$
EQ	HA	UA	LT	LF	OT	HE	SQ	UA	RE	RO
$6\sqrt{3}$	$5\sqrt{3}$	25	$3\sqrt{3}$	$6\sqrt{3}$	5	20	3	$3\sqrt{3}$	36	2
OT	OF	TH	ER	AD	IU	EH	SO	FT	YP	PY
11	4	16	6	8	32	$5\sqrt{2}$	2	7	$8\sqrt{3}$	$2\sqrt{2}$
OT	TH	EN	AG	OR	US	AS	TH	E.	T.	S.

In a 30–60 degrees right triangle, the side opposite the 30-degree angle is

_ _ _ _   _ _ _   _ _ _ _ _ _ _ _

Right Triangle Trigonometry

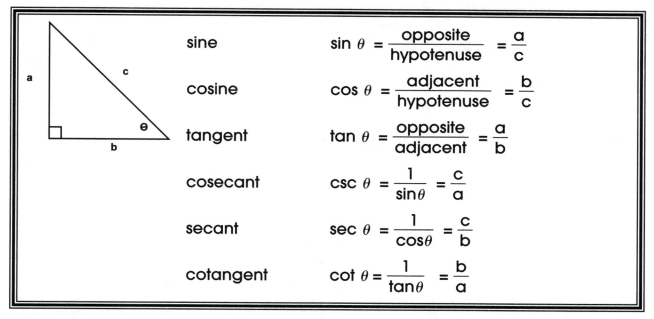

sine	$\sin \theta = \dfrac{\text{opposite}}{\text{hypotenuse}} = \dfrac{a}{c}$	
cosine	$\cos \theta = \dfrac{\text{adjacent}}{\text{hypotenuse}} = \dfrac{b}{c}$	
tangent	$\tan \theta = \dfrac{\text{opposite}}{\text{adjacent}} = \dfrac{a}{b}$	
cosecant	$\csc \theta = \dfrac{1}{\sin\theta} = \dfrac{c}{a}$	
secant	$\sec \theta = \dfrac{1}{\cos\theta} = \dfrac{c}{b}$	
cotangent	$\cot \theta = \dfrac{1}{\tan\theta} = \dfrac{b}{a}$	

Find the six trigonometric functions for the angles below.

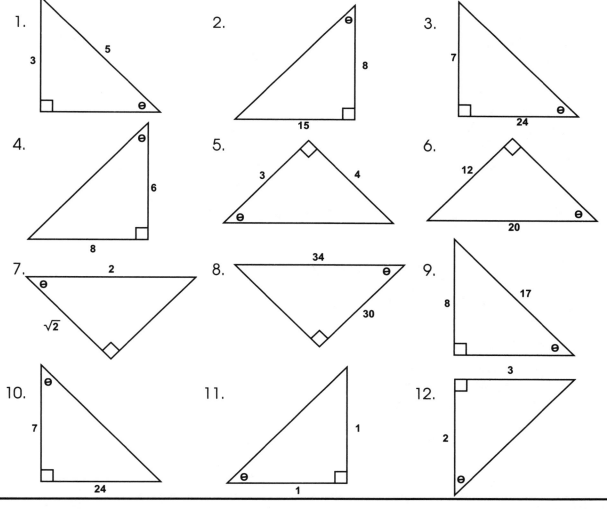

Solving Any Triangle

$$\tan \theta = \frac{\sin \theta}{\cos \theta}$$

$$\sin (^-\theta) = -\sin \theta \qquad \cos (^-\theta) = \cos\theta$$

$$\cos (\theta + \beta) = \cos\theta \cos \beta - \sin \theta \sin \beta$$

$$\sin (\theta + \beta) = \sin\theta \cos \beta + \cos \theta \sin \beta$$

$$\cos \frac{\pi}{2} = 0 \qquad \sin \frac{\pi}{2} = 1 \qquad \tan \frac{\pi}{2} \text{ is undefined}$$

$$\cos \pi = {}^-1 \qquad \sin \pi = 0 \qquad \tan \pi = 0$$

$$\cos (\theta - \beta) = \cos (\theta + (^-\beta))$$
$$= \cos (\theta) \cos (^-\beta) - \sin (\theta) \sin (^-\beta)$$
$$= \cos \theta \cos \beta - \sin \theta (-\sin \beta)$$
$$\cos (\theta - \beta) = \cos \theta \cos \beta + \sin \theta \sin \beta$$

Evaluate the following using the above identities.

1. $\sin (\theta - \beta)$

2. $\tan (\theta + \beta)$

3. $\tan (\theta - \beta)$

4. $\cos (\theta + \frac{\pi}{2})$

5. $\cos (\theta + \pi)$

6. $\sin (\theta + \frac{\pi}{2})$

7. $\sin (\theta + \pi)$

8. $\sin (2\theta)$

9. $\cos (2\theta)$

10. $\tan (2\theta)$

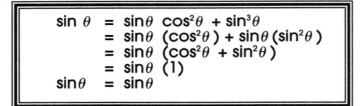

$$\sin \theta = \sin\theta \cos^2\theta + \sin^3\theta$$
$$= \sin\theta (\cos^2\theta) + \sin\theta (\sin^2\theta)$$
$$= \sin\theta (\cos^2\theta + \sin^2\theta)$$
$$= \sin\theta (1)$$
$$\sin\theta = \sin\theta$$

Verify the following identities.

1. $\csc^2\theta = 1 + \cot^2\theta$

2. $\sec^2\theta = 1 + \tan^2\theta$

3. $\cos\theta = \sec\theta - \tan\theta \sin\theta$

4. $\sin\theta = \csc\theta - \cot\theta \cos\theta$

Name _____   Date _____

Solving Any Triangle

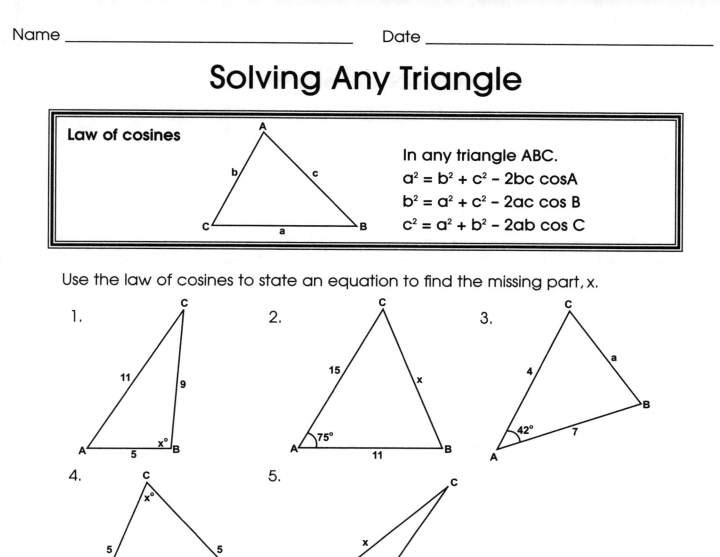

Law of cosines

In any triangle ABC.
$$a^2 = b^2 + c^2 - 2bc \cos A$$
$$b^2 = a^2 + c^2 - 2ac \cos B$$
$$c^2 = a^2 + b^2 - 2ab \cos C$$

Use the law of cosines to state an equation to find the missing part, x.

1.

2.

3.

4.

5.

Find the indicated part of ΔABC. Round angles to the nearest tenth and lengths to three significant digits.

6. $b = 12, c = 10, \angle A = 38°, a = $ _____

7. $a = 14, b = 15, c = 18, \angle A = $ _____

8. $a = 12, c = 11, \angle B = 81°, b = $ _____

9. $a = 8, b = 9, c = 15, \angle C = $ _____

10. $a = 5, b = 7, \angle C = 40°, c = $ _____

11. $c = 20, b = 30, \angle A = 140°, a = $ _____

12. $b = 2, a = 4, \angle C = 20°, c = $ _____

13. $a = 5, b = 9, c = 11, \angle C = $ _____

14. $a = 1.5, b = 3, c = 2, \angle B = $ _____

15. $a = .6, b = .8, c = 1.2, \angle A = $ _____

0-7424-1776-X *Geometry*

Laws of Sines

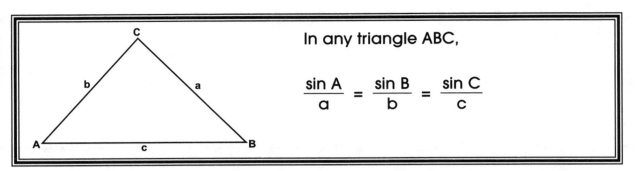

In any triangle ABC,

$$\frac{\sin A}{a} = \frac{\sin B}{b} = \frac{\sin C}{c}$$

Use the law of sines to state an equation to find the missing part, x.

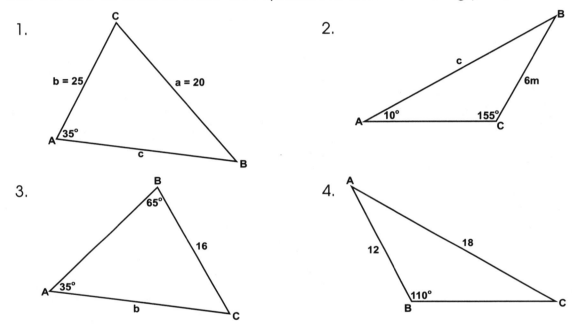

1.

b = 25   a = 20

35°

c

2.

c

6m

10°   155°

3.

65°

16

35°

b

4.

12   18

110°

Find the indicated part of △ABC. Round angles to the nearest tenth and lengths to three significant digits.

5. c = 10, ∠A = 48°, ∠C = 63°, a = _____

6. a = 20, b = 15, ∠A = 40°, ∠B = _____

7. a = 40, b = 50, ∠A = 37°, ∠B = _____

8. a = 11, c = 15, ∠A = 40°, ∠C = _____

9. c = 30, ∠A = 42°, ∠C = 98°, a = _____

10. a = 1.5, b = 2.0, ∠B = 35°, ∠A = _____

11. a = 16, ∠A = 35°, ∠C = 65°, c = _____

12. b = 18, c = 32, ∠C = 100°, ∠B = _____

Properties of Parallelograms

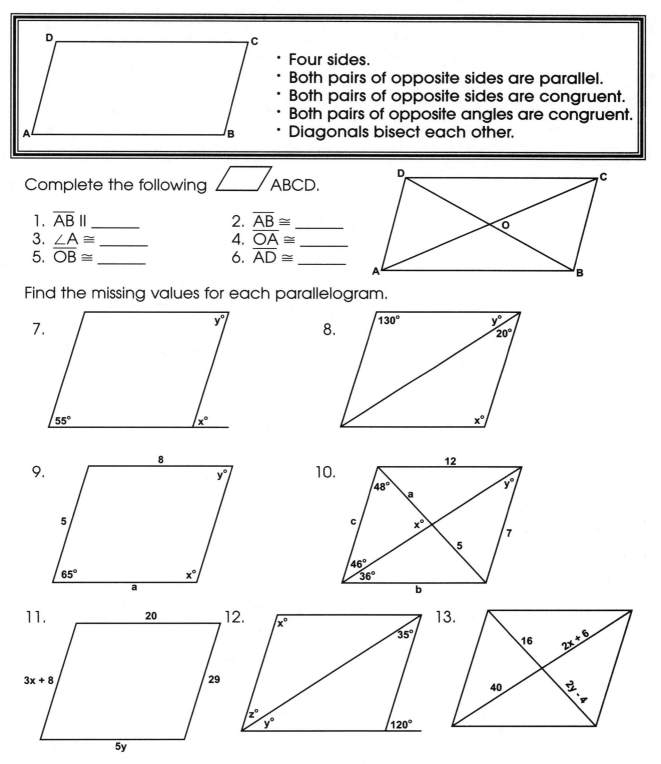

- Four sides.
- Both pairs of opposite sides are parallel.
- Both pairs of opposite sides are congruent.
- Both pairs of opposite angles are congruent.
- Diagonals bisect each other.

Complete the following ▱ ABCD.

1. $\overline{AB}$ ∥ _____
2. $\overline{AB}$ ≅ _____
3. ∠A ≅ _____
4. $\overline{OA}$ ≅ _____
5. $\overline{OB}$ ≅ _____
6. $\overline{AD}$ ≅ _____

Find the missing values for each parallelogram.

7. 55°, $y°$, $x°$

8. 130°, $y°$, 20°, $x°$

9. 8, 5, 65°, $y°$, $x°$, a

10. 12, 48°, a, c, $x°$, 46°, 36°, 5, 7, $y°$, b

11. 20, 3x + 8, 29, 5y

12. $x°$, 35°, $z°$, $y°$, 120°

13. 16, 2x + 6, 40, 2y - 4

Two-Column Proofs: Parallelograms

> **Five Ways to Prove that a Quadrilateral is a Parallelogram**
> 1. Show both pairs of opposite sides are parallel.
> 2. Show both pairs of opposite sides are congruent.
> 3. Show one pair of opposite sides are both congruent and parallel.
> 4. Show both pairs of opposite angles are congruent.
> 5. Show that diagonals bisect each other.

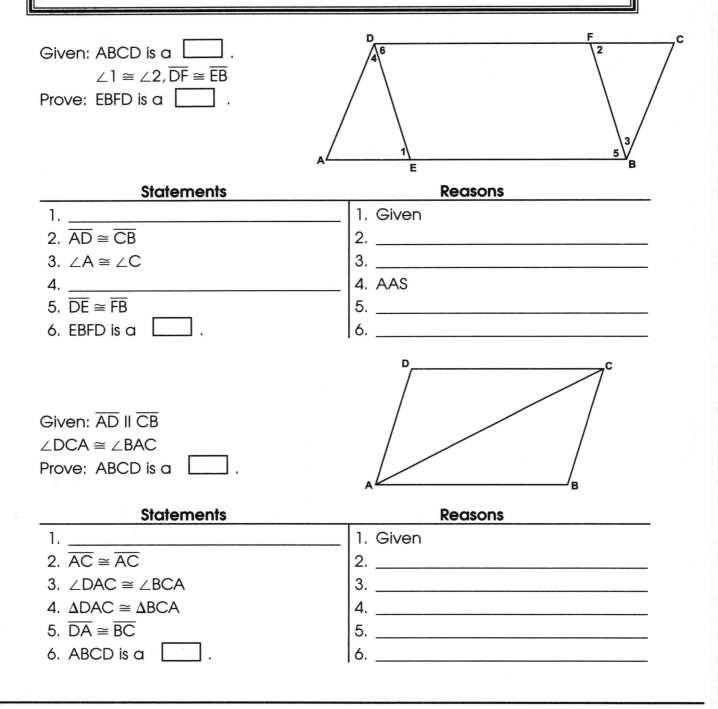

Given: ABCD is a ☐ .
  $\angle 1 \cong \angle 2, \overline{DF} \cong \overline{EB}$
Prove: EBFD is a ☐ .

Statements	Reasons
1. _____	1. Given
2. $\overline{AD} \cong \overline{CB}$	2. _____
3. $\angle A \cong \angle C$	3. _____
4. _____	4. AAS
5. $\overline{DE} \cong \overline{FB}$	5. _____
6. EBFD is a ☐ .	6. _____

Given: $\overline{AD} \parallel \overline{CB}$
$\angle DCA \cong \angle BAC$
Prove: ABCD is a ☐ .

Statements	Reasons
1. _____	1. Given
2. $\overline{AC} \cong \overline{AC}$	2. _____
3. $\angle DAC \cong \angle BCA$	3. _____
4. $\triangle DAC \cong \triangle BCA$	4. _____
5. $\overline{DA} \cong \overline{BC}$	5. _____
6. ABCD is a ☐ .	6. _____

More Two-Column Proofs: Parallelograms

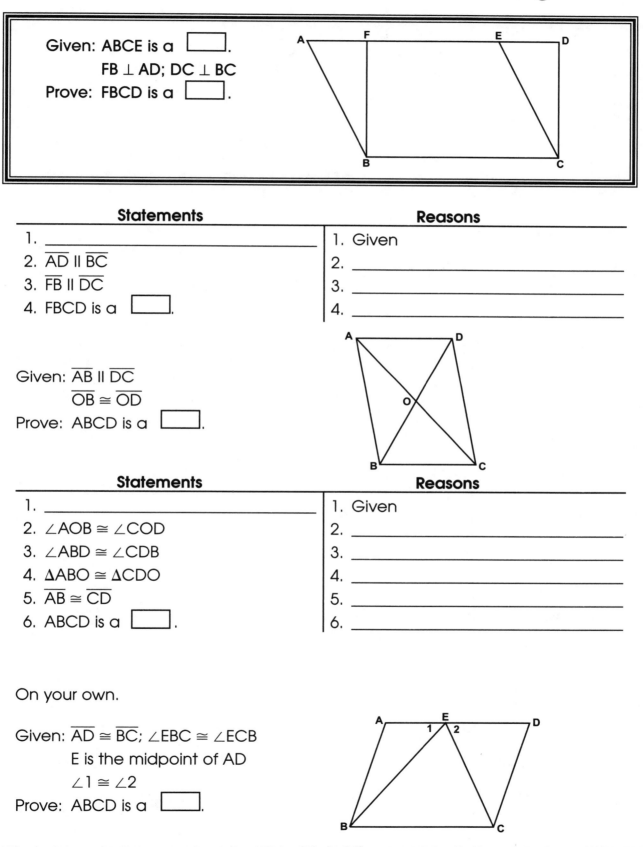

Given: ABCE is a ☐.
       FB ⊥ AD; DC ⊥ BC
Prove: FBCD is a ☐.

Statements	Reasons
1. _____	1. Given
2. $\overline{AD}$ ‖ $\overline{BC}$	2. _____
3. $\overline{FB}$ ‖ $\overline{DC}$	3. _____
4. FBCD is a ☐.	4. _____

Given: $\overline{AB}$ ‖ $\overline{DC}$
       $\overline{OB}$ ≅ $\overline{OD}$
Prove: ABCD is a ☐.

Statements	Reasons
1. _____	1. Given
2. ∠AOB ≅ ∠COD	2. _____
3. ∠ABD ≅ ∠CDB	3. _____
4. △ABO ≅ △CDO	4. _____
5. $\overline{AB}$ ≅ $\overline{CD}$	5. _____
6. ABCD is a ☐.	6. _____

On your own.

Given: $\overline{AD}$ ≅ $\overline{BC}$; ∠EBC ≅ ∠ECB
       E is the midpoint of AD
       ∠1 ≅ ∠2
Prove: ABCD is a ☐.

Special Parallelograms

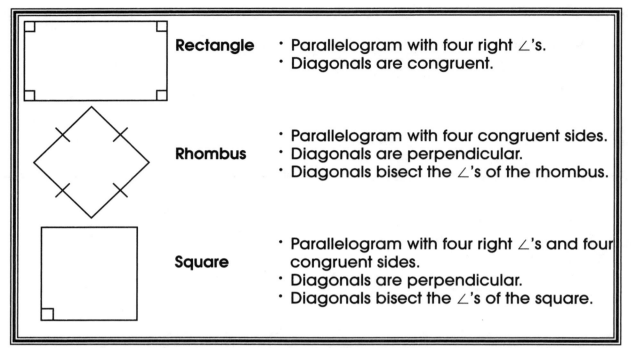

Rectangle
- Parallelogram with four right ∠'s.
- Diagonals are congruent.

Rhombus
- Parallelogram with four congruent sides.
- Diagonals are perpendicular.
- Diagonals bisect the ∠'s of the rhombus.

Square
- Parallelogram with four right ∠'s and four congruent sides.
- Diagonals are perpendicular.
- Diagonals bisect the ∠'s of the square.

In problems 1-8, list the letters of the quadrilaterals that the property holds true for: a) Parallelogram   b) Rectangle   c) Rhombus   d) Square

1. Diagonals bisect each other.
2. All ∠'s are right ∠'s.
3. All sides are congruent.
4. Opposite sides are congruent.
5. Opposite angles are congruent.
6. Diagonals are congruent.
7. Diagonals are perpendicular.
8. Opposite sides are parallel.

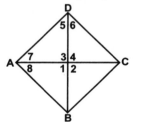

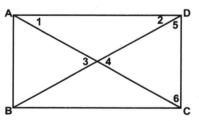

9. ABCD is a rhombus. If m∠8 = 35, find the measures of ∠1, ∠2, ∠3, ∠4, ∠5, ∠6, ∠7.

10. ABCD is a rectangle. If m∠1 = 20, find the measures of ∠2, ∠3, ∠4, ∠5, ∠6.

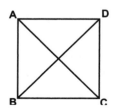

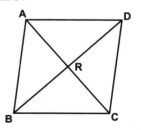

11. ABCD is a square. If $\overline{AC}$ = 16 and $\overline{BD}$ = 2x + 4, find x.

12. ABCD is a parallelogram. $\overline{AR}$ = 2x + 3, $\overline{RC}$ = 35, $\overline{BR}$ = 4y − 10 $\overline{DR}$ = 90. Find x and y.

0-7424-1776-X *Geometry*

Trapezoids

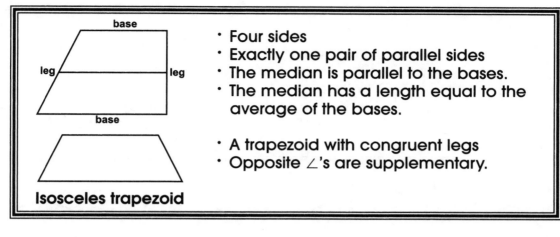

- Four sides
- Exactly one pair of parallel sides
- The median is parallel to the bases.
- The median has a length equal to the average of the bases.

- A trapezoid with congruent legs
- Opposite ∠'s are supplementary.

Isosceles trapezoid

Find the missing values.

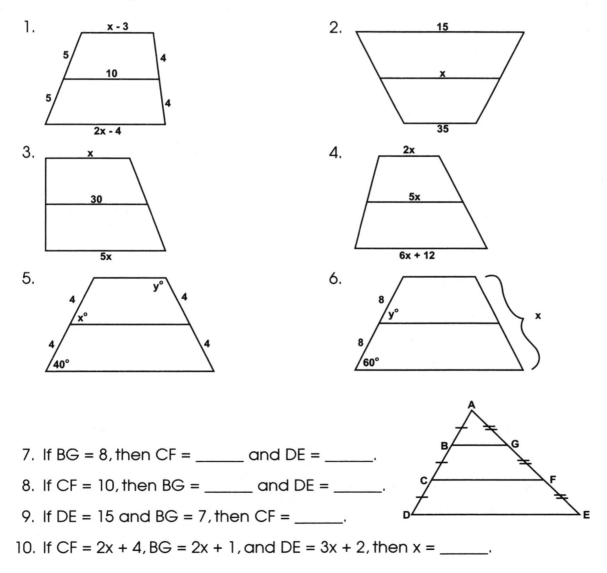

7. If BG = 8, then CF = _____ and DE = _____.

8. If CF = 10, then BG = _____ and DE = _____.

9. If DE = 15 and BG = 7, then CF = _____.

10. If CF = 2x + 4, BG = 2x + 1, and DE = 3x + 2, then x = _____.

Circumference and Area

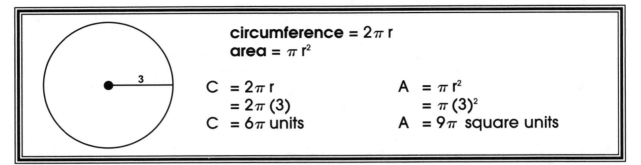

circumference = $2\pi r$
area = πr^2

C = $2\pi r$	A = πr^2
= $2\pi (3)$	= $\pi (3)^2$
C = 6π units	A = 9π square units

Find the circumference and area of each circle.

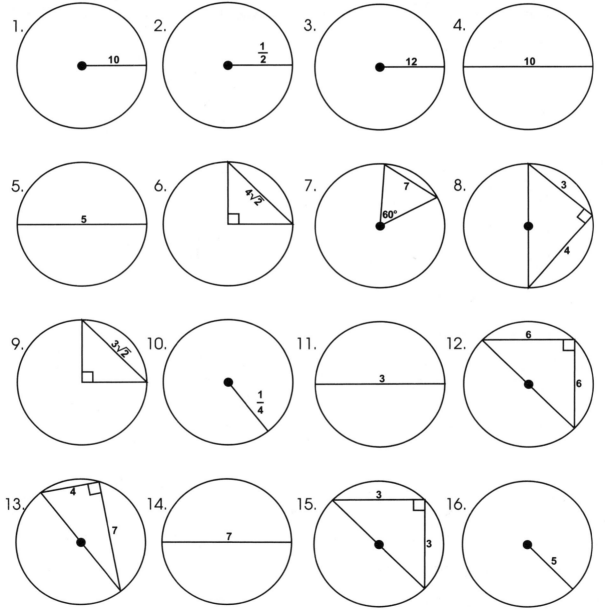

Draw, Fold, But Don't Spindle

Several geometric shapes can be drawn or folded using simple materials.

Circle: Thumbtack, string, cardboard, pencil
1. Place the thumbtack in the center of the cardboard.
2. Tie a string in a loop that when pulled taut is the length of the radius.
3. Place the loop around the thumbtack and pull the loop taut with the pencil.
4. Draw the circle keeping the loop taut.

Why: A circle is a set of points a given distance (radius) from a point (center).

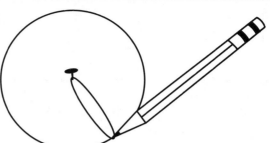

Ellipse: 2 thumbtacks, string, cardboard, pencil
1. Place 2 thumbtacks (foci) two inches apart on the cardboard.
2. Tie a string in a loop that when pulled taut is four inches in length.
3. Place the loop around the thumbtacks and pencil. Pull the loop taut with the pencil.
4. Draw the ellipse keeping the loop taut.

Why: An ellipse is the set of points in which the sum of the distances from the foci is a constant.

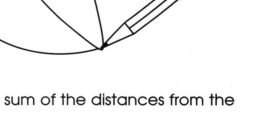

Ellipse: Thin paper or wax paper, ruler, pencil
1. Draw a three-inch radius circle. Mark the center.
2. Draw a point A two inches from the center.
3. Fold and crease the paper so a point on the circle touches point A.
4. Make about 40 folds around the circle.

Why: The sum of the distance from the fold to the center and the fold to point A is constant.

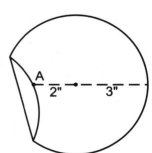

Parabola: Thin paper or wax paper, ruler, pencil
1. Draw a point (focus).
2. Draw a line parallel to the bottom of the paper.
3. Fold and crease the paper about 40 times so the line touches the point.

Why: A parabola is the set of points equidistant from a point and a line.

Nets: All Wrapped Up

A **net** is a pattern that can be folded to cover a solid figure. The area of the net equals the surface area of the solid.

Match the net with its solid and find the the surface area. (Assume each square is 1 cm².)

1. _____ Area = _____ 2. _____ Area = _____ 3. _____ Area = _____

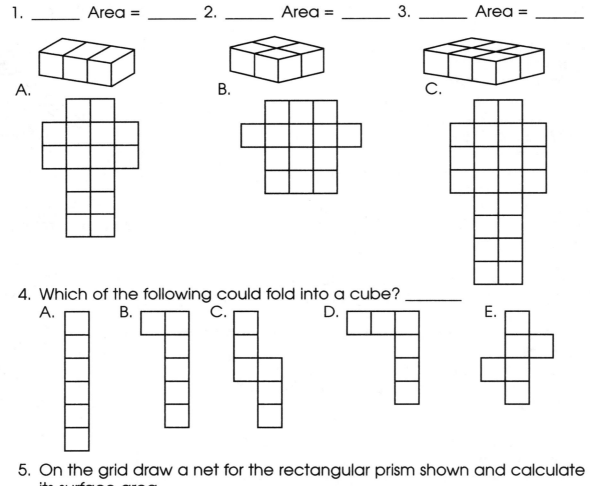

4. Which of the following could fold into a cube? _____

A.   B.   C.   D.   E.

5. On the grid draw a net for the rectangular prism shown and calculate its surface area.

Prism   Net   Area _____

Painting the Cube Red

Assume a cube is painted red and is cut into unit cubes. Use the figures below to complete the table.

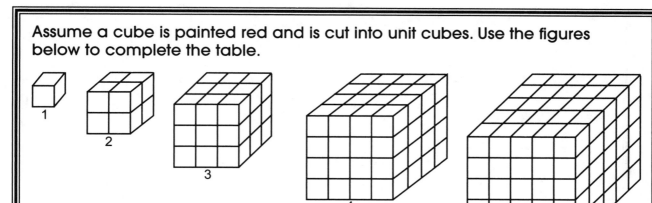

Length of one edge	No. of unit cubes with 3 red faces	No. of unit cubes with 2 red faces	No. of unit cubes with 1 red face	No. of unit cubes with 0 red faces
2				
3				
4				
5				

Consider the pattern of each column in order to complete the following table.

Length of one edge	No. of unit cubes with 3 red faces	No. of unit cubes with 2 red faces	No. of unit cubes with 1 red face	No. of unit cubes with 0 red faces
6				
7				
8				
9				
10				

Describe the sequence of numbers in each column.

3 red faces: _____

2 red faces: _____

1 red faces: _____

0 red faces: _____

0-7424-1776-X *Geometry*

Sectors and Arcs

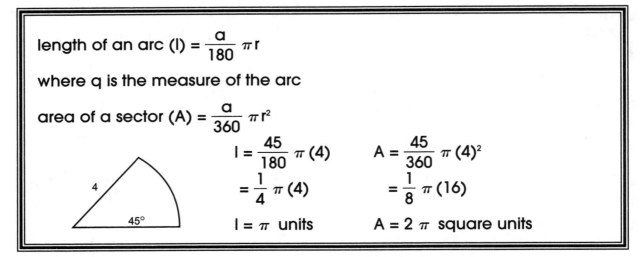

length of an arc (l) = $\dfrac{a}{180}\, \pi\, r$

where q is the measure of the arc

area of a sector (A) = $\dfrac{a}{360}\, \pi\, r^2$

$l = \dfrac{45}{180}\, \pi\, (4)$ $A = \dfrac{45}{360}\, \pi\, (4)^2$

$= \dfrac{1}{4}\, \pi\, (4)$ $= \dfrac{1}{8}\, \pi\, (16)$

$l = \pi$ units $A = 2\, \pi$ square units

Find the length of each arc and the area of each sector.

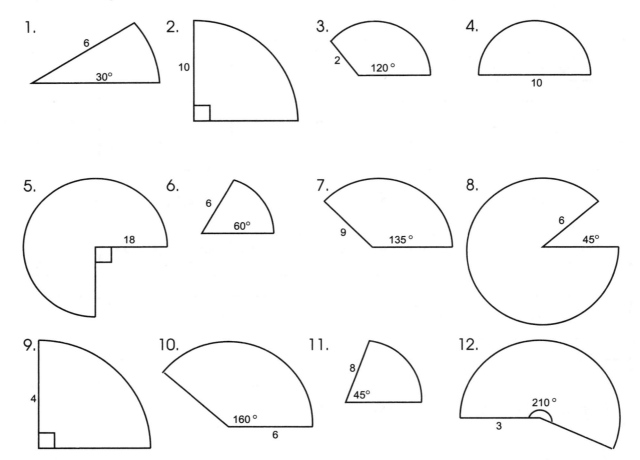

Just for Fun: Networks

Draw each figure without lifting your pencil from the paper and without tracing any line more than once.

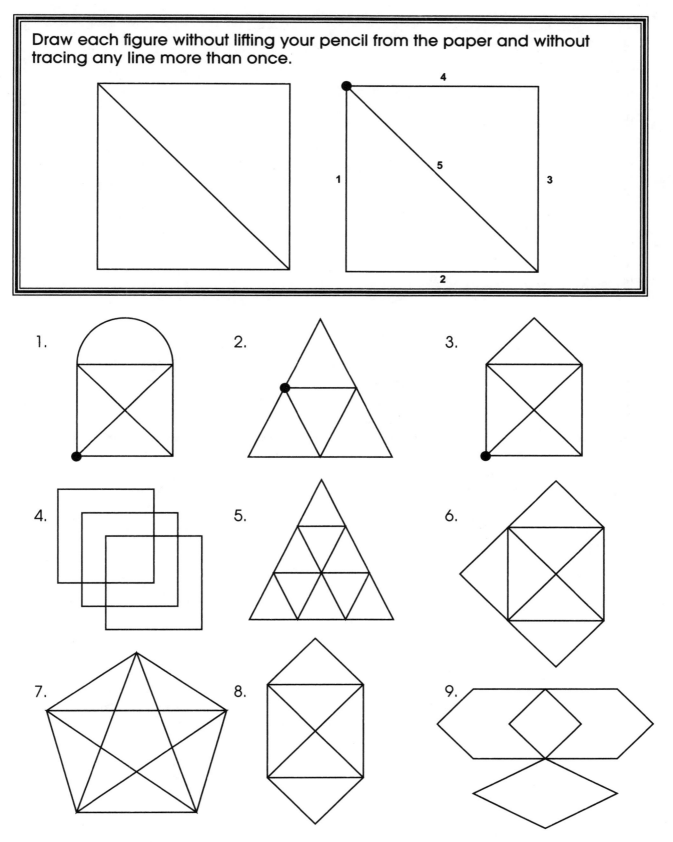

Tangents, Secants, and Chords

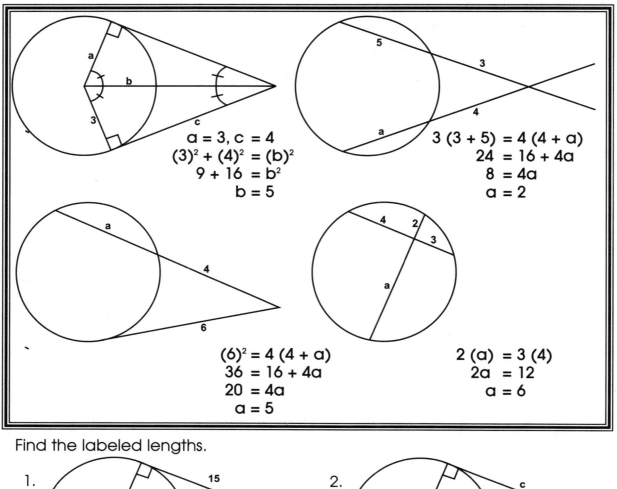

$a = 3, c = 4$
$(3)^2 + (4)^2 = (b)^2$
$9 + 16 = b^2$
$b = 5$

$3 (3 + 5) = 4 (4 + a)$
$24 = 16 + 4a$
$8 = 4a$
$a = 2$

$(6)^2 = 4 (4 + a)$
$36 = 16 + 4a$
$20 = 4a$
$a = 5$

$2 (a) = 3 (4)$
$2a = 12$
$a = 6$

Find the labeled lengths.

1.

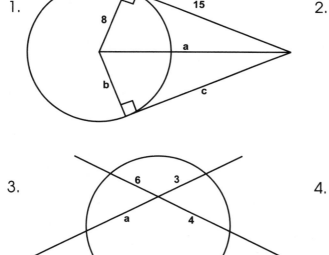

2.

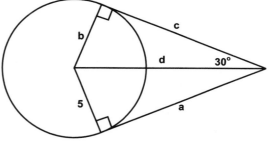

3.

4.

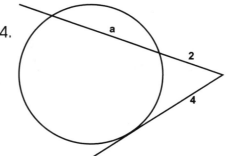

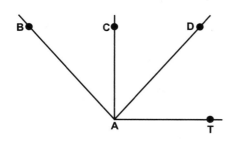

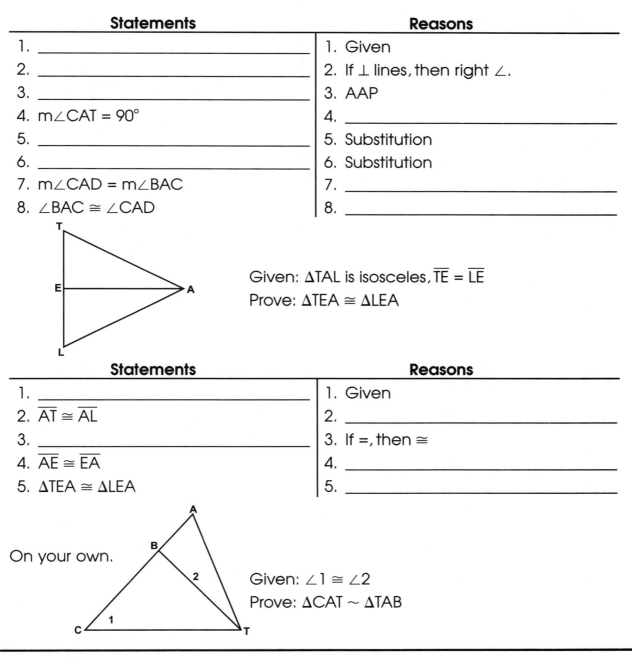

More Two-Column Proofs

Complete the following proofs.

Given: $\overline{CA} \perp \overline{AT}$, $m\angle BAC + m\angle DAT = 90°$
Prove: $\angle BAC \cong \angle CAD$

Statements	Reasons
1. _____	1. Given
2. _____	2. If ⊥ lines, then right ∠.
3. _____	3. AAP
4. $m\angle CAT = 90°$	4. _____
5. _____	5. Substitution
6. _____	6. Substitution
7. $m\angle CAD = m\angle BAC$	7. _____
8. $\angle BAC \cong \angle CAD$	8. _____

Given: ΔTAL is isosceles, $\overline{TE} = \overline{LE}$
Prove: $\Delta TEA \cong \Delta LEA$

Statements	Reasons
1. _____	1. Given
2. $\overline{AT} \cong \overline{AL}$	2. _____
3. _____	3. If =, then ≅
4. $\overline{AE} \cong \overline{EA}$	4. _____
5. $\Delta TEA \cong \Delta LEA$	5. _____

On your own.

Given: $\angle 1 \cong \angle 2$
Prove: $\Delta CAT \sim \Delta TAB$

More Practice with Proofs

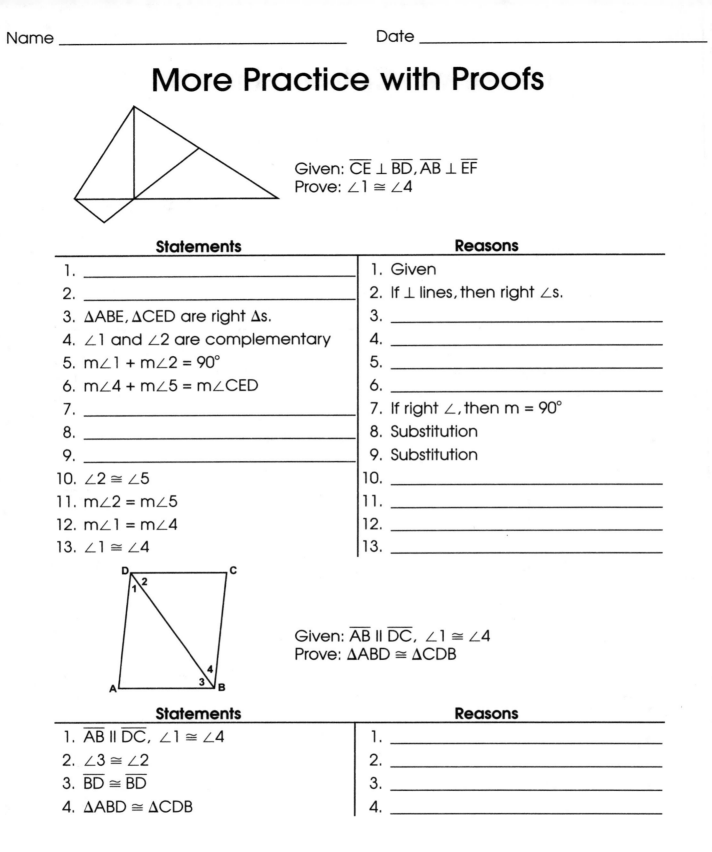

Given: $\overline{CE} \perp \overline{BD}, \overline{AB} \perp \overline{EF}$
Prove: $\angle 1 \cong \angle 4$

Statements	Reasons
1. _____	1. Given
2. _____	2. If $\perp$ lines, then right $\angle$s.
3. $\triangle ABE, \triangle CED$ are right $\triangle$s.	3. _____
4. $\angle 1$ and $\angle 2$ are complementary	4. _____
5. $m\angle 1 + m\angle 2 = 90°$	5. _____
6. $m\angle 4 + m\angle 5 = m\angle CED$	6. _____
7. _____	7. If right $\angle$, then m = 90°
8. _____	8. Substitution
9. _____	9. Substitution
10. $\angle 2 \cong \angle 5$	10. _____
11. $m\angle 2 = m\angle 5$	11. _____
12. $m\angle 1 = m\angle 4$	12. _____
13. $\angle 1 \cong \angle 4$	13. _____

Given: $\overline{AB} \parallel \overline{DC}, \angle 1 \cong \angle 4$
Prove: $\triangle ABD \cong \triangle CDB$

Statements	Reasons
1. $\overline{AB} \parallel \overline{DC}, \angle 1 \cong \angle 4$	1. _____
2. $\angle 3 \cong \angle 2$	2. _____
3. $\overline{BD} \cong \overline{BD}$	3. _____
4. $\triangle ABD \cong \triangle CDB$	4. _____

Polygonal Regions

A **polygonal region** is defined to be the union of a finite number of triangular regions in a single plane. The intersection of any two or more triangular regions is either a point or a segment.

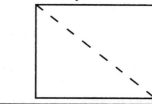

This is polygonal region.

Determine if each region below is polygonal by breaking it into triangular regions.

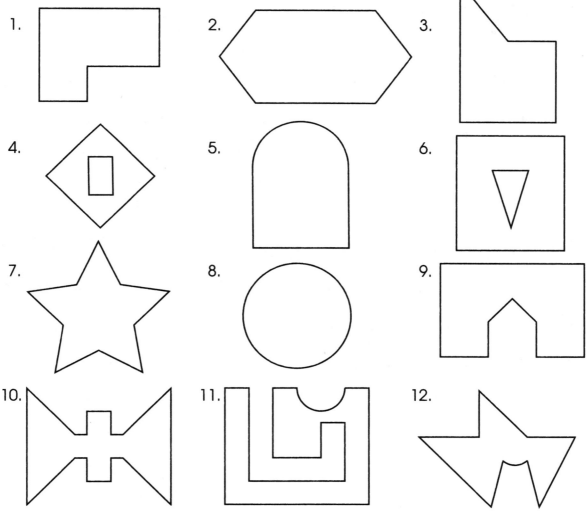

1.

2.

3.

4.

5.

6.

7.

8.

9.

10.

11.

12.

Polygons

Types of Polygons

Number of Sides	Name
3	triangle
4	quadrilateral
5	pentagon
6	hexagon
8	octagon
10	decagon
n	n-gon

- A regular polygon has equal angles and equal sides.
- The sum of the measures of the angles of a convex polygon with n sides is $(n - 2)\,180°$.
- The sum of the measures of the exterior angles of any convex polygon is $360°$.

Find the following for each polygon: a) The sum of the measures of the interior angles, b) The sum of the measures of the exterior angles.

1. A 32-sided polygon
2. A 12-sided polygon
3. A 6-sided polygon
4. An 8-sided polygon
5. A 3-sided polygon
6. A 5-sided polygon

Find the following for each regular polygon: a) The measure of each exterior angle, b) the measure of each interior angle.

7. A 6-sided polygon
8. A 5-sided polygon
9. A 3-sided polygon
10. An 8-sided polygon
11. A 4-sided polygon
12. A 10-sided polygon

13. A regular polygon has an exterior angle with a measure of 20°. Find the number of sides.

14. A regular polygon has an interior angle with a measure of 120°. Find the number of sides.

15. A regular polygon has 20 sides. Find the measure of each exterior angle.

16. A regular polygon has 10 sides. Find the measure of each interior angle.

Perimeter

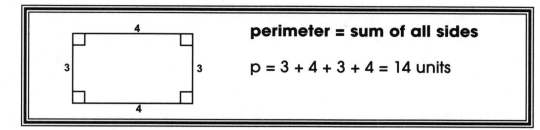

perimeter = sum of all sides

p = 3 + 4 + 3 + 4 = 14 units

Find the perimeter of the polygonal regions below.

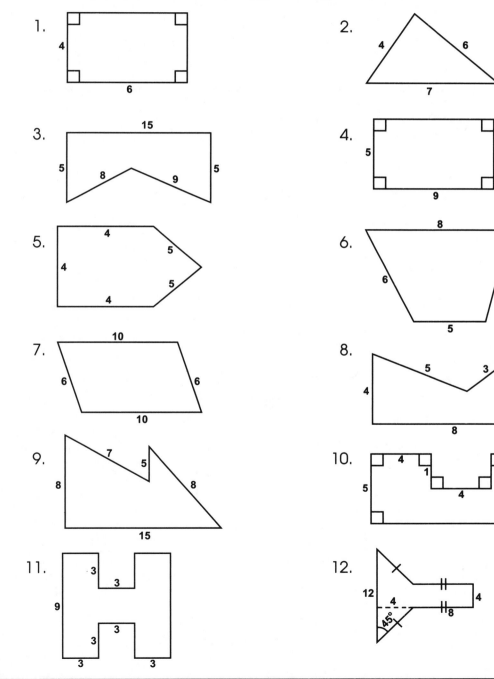

1.

2.

3.

4.

5.

6.

7.

8.

9.

10.

11.

12.

Area

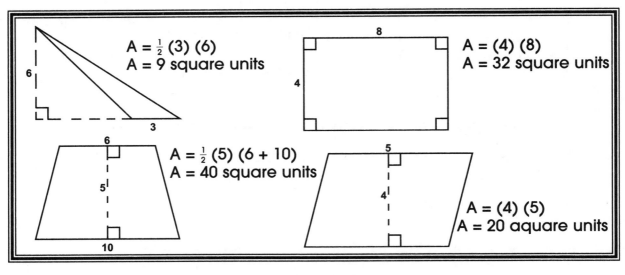

$A = \frac{1}{2}$ (3) (6)
$A = 9$ square units

$A = (4)$ (8)
$A = 32$ square units

$A = \frac{1}{2}$ (5) (6 + 10)
$A = 40$ square units

$A = (4)$ (5)
$A = 20$ aquare units

Find the areas of the polygonal regions below.

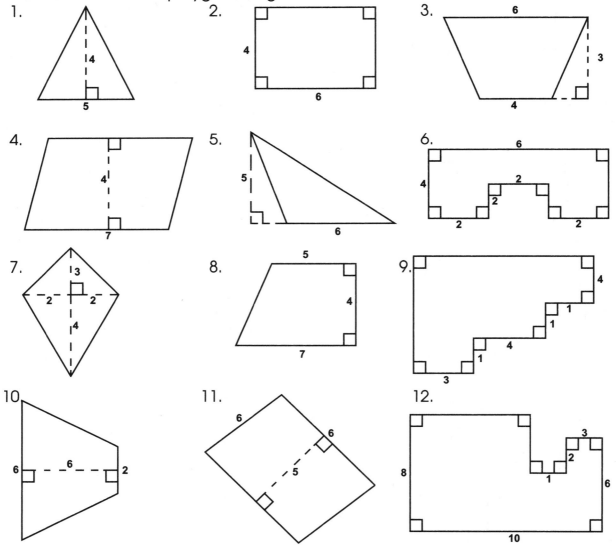

Regular Polygons

A **regular polygon** is a convex polygon with all sides congruent and all angles congruent.

apothem (a) = distance from the center of the polygon to a side

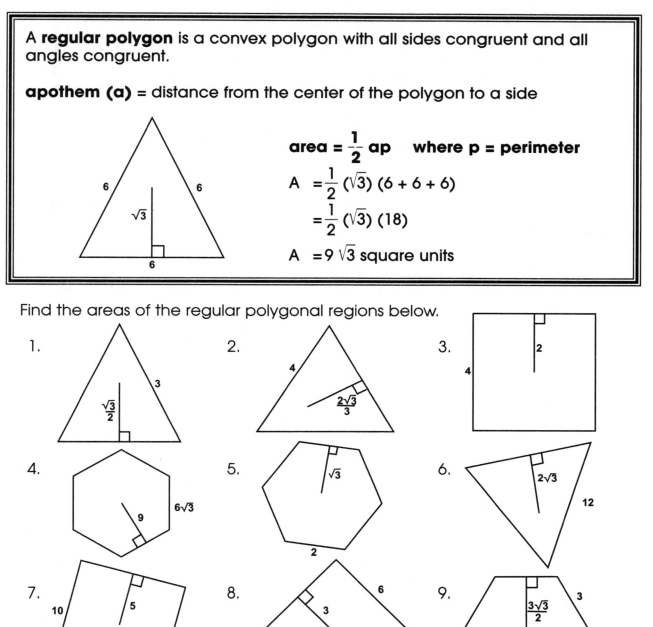

area = $\frac{1}{2}$ ap   where p = perimeter

$A = \frac{1}{2} (\sqrt{3})(6 + 6 + 6)$

$= \frac{1}{2} (\sqrt{3})(18)$

$A = 9\sqrt{3}$ square units

Find the areas of the regular polygonal regions below.

1. $\frac{\sqrt{3}}{2}$ 3

2.   4 $\frac{2\sqrt{3}}{3}$

3.   4   2

4.   9 $6\sqrt{3}$

5. $\sqrt{3}$ 2

6. $2\sqrt{3}$ 12

7.   10   5

8.   3   6

9. $\frac{3\sqrt{3}}{2}$ 3

10.   3 $6\sqrt{3}$

11.   2   8

12. $\frac{2}{3}\sqrt{3}$ 1

Prisms

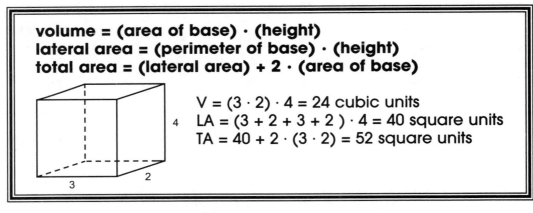

volume = (area of base) · (height)
lateral area = (perimeter of base) · (height)
total area = (lateral area) + 2 · (area of base)

V = (3 · 2) · 4 = 24 cubic units
LA = (3 + 2 + 3 + 2) · 4 = 40 square units
TA = 40 + 2 · (3 · 2) = 52 square units

Find the volume, lateral area, and total area of the following prisms.

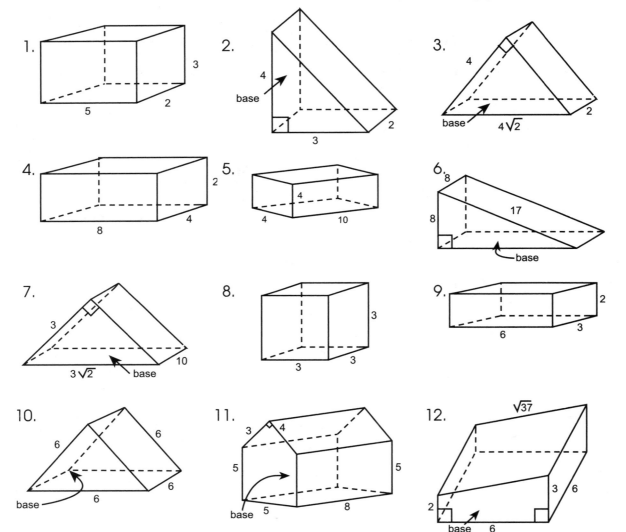

Right Circular Cylinders

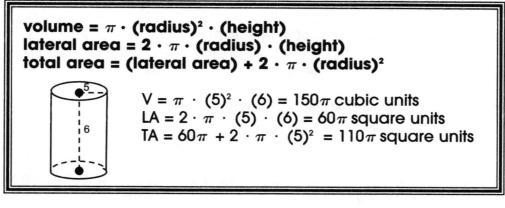

volume = $\pi \cdot$ (radius)$^2 \cdot$ (height)
lateral area = 2 $\cdot \pi \cdot$ (radius) $\cdot$ (height)
total area = (lateral area) + 2 $\cdot \pi \cdot$ (radius)^2

$V = \pi \cdot (5)^2 \cdot (6) = 150\pi$ cubic units
$LA = 2 \cdot \pi \cdot (5) \cdot (6) = 60\pi$ square units
$TA = 60\pi + 2 \cdot \pi \cdot (5)^2 = 110\pi$ square units

Find the volume, lateral area, and total area of the following right circular cylinders.

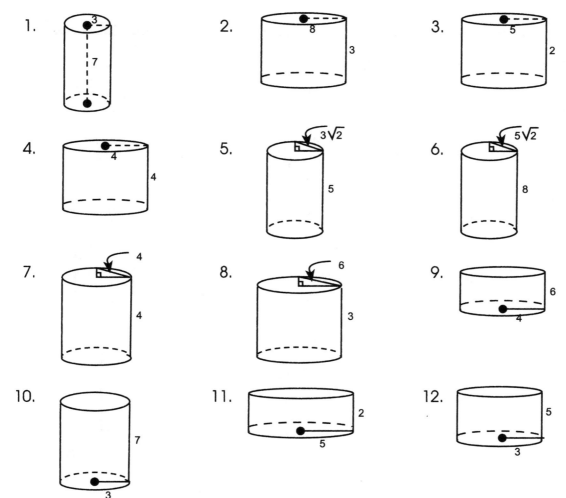

1.

2.

3.

4.

5.

6.

7.

8.

9.

10.

11.

12.

Pyramids

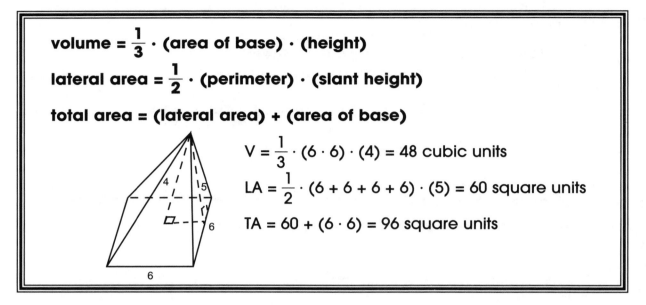

volume = $\frac{1}{3}$ · (area of base) · (height)

lateral area = $\frac{1}{2}$ · (perimeter) · (slant height)

total area = (lateral area) + (area of base)

$V = \frac{1}{3} \cdot (6 \cdot 6) \cdot (4) = 48$ cubic units

$LA = \frac{1}{2} \cdot (6 + 6 + 6 + 6) \cdot (5) = 60$ square units

$TA = 60 + (6 \cdot 6) = 96$ square units

Find the volume, lateral area, and total area of the following pyramids.

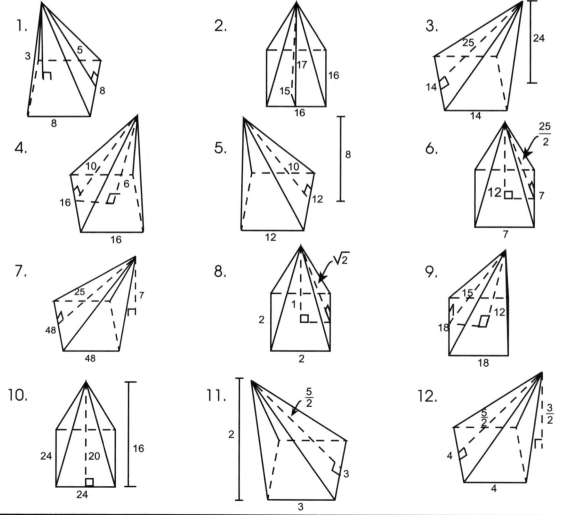

1. 3, 5, 8, 8

2. 17, 15, 16, 16

3. 25, 24, 14, 14

4. 10, 6, 16, 16

5. 10, 8, 12, 12

6. $\frac{25}{2}$, 12, 7, 7

7. 25, 7, 48, 48

8. $\sqrt{2}$, 1, 2, 2

9. 15, 12, 18, 18

10. 24, 20, 16, 24

11. $\frac{5}{2}$, 2, 3, 3

12. $\frac{5}{2}$, $\frac{3}{2}$, 4, 4

0-7424-1776-X *Geometry*

Right Circular Cones

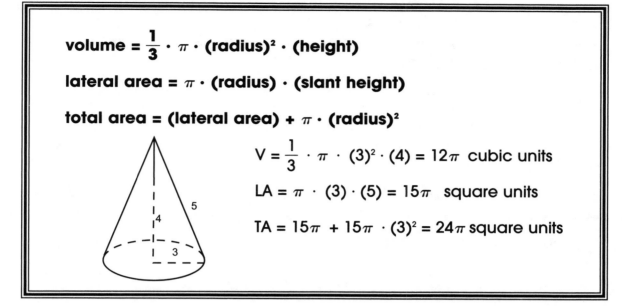

volume = $\frac{1}{3} \cdot \pi \cdot$ **(radius)² · (height)**

lateral area = $\pi \cdot$ **(radius) · (slant height)**

total area = **(lateral area)** + $\pi \cdot$ **(radius)²**

$V = \frac{1}{3} \cdot \pi \cdot (3)^2 \cdot (4) = 12\pi$ cubic units

$LA = \pi \cdot (3) \cdot (5) = 15\pi$ square units

$TA = 15\pi + 15\pi \cdot (3)^2 = 24\pi$ square units

Find the volume, lateral area, and total area of the following right circular cones.

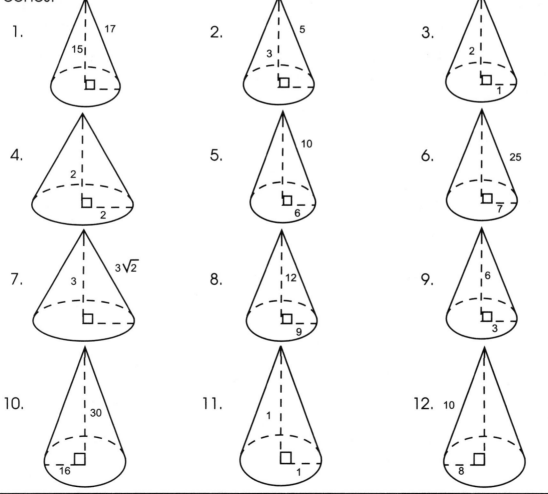

1. 17, 15, □

2. 5, 3, □

3. 2, □, 1

4. 2, □, 2

5. 10, □, 6

6. 25, □, 7

7. 3, $3\sqrt{2}$, □

8. 12, □, 9

9. 6, □, 3

10. 30, □, 16

11. 1, □, 1

12. 10, □, 8

Platonic Solids

A polyhedron is **regular** if all faces of the solid are congruent regular polygons and the same number of polygons meet at each vertex. There are only 5 regular polyhedra—the Platonic Solids.

tetrahedron   octahedron   icosahedron   cube   dodecahedron

Use the following steps to make a Platonic Solid.
1. Cut out the circle to use as a pattern.
2. Cut out the number of circles equal to the number of faces of the Platonic Solid you are making: Tetrahedron, 4; octahedron, 8; icosahedron, 20; cube, 6; dodecahedron, 12.
3. Trace the inscribed polygon onto stiff paper to use as a folding template. Use the polygon corresponding to the shape of the face of the Platonic Solid. Triangle-tetrahedron, octahedron, icosahedron. Square-cube Pentagon-dodecahedron
4. Place the template on each circle and fold back the flaps.
5. Glue or staple flaps of the faces at each vertex to make the Platonic Solid.

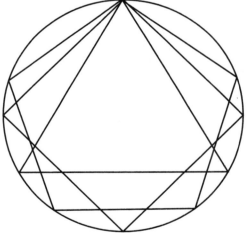

Historical Comment: The Platonic Solids are named after Plato, a Greek philosopher and mathematician (427-347 B.C.). In ancient Greece, the four basic elements were identified with four of the Platonic Solids: tetrahedron, fire; cube, earth; octahedron, air; and icosahedron, water. The dodecahedron with its 12 faces was related to the universe (12 signs of the zodiac).

Name _____ Date _____

Logic: If..., Then...

Conditional p→q	Statement If p, then q. If it rains, you use an umbrella.
Converse q→p	If q, then p. If you use an umbrella, then it rains.
Inverse ~ p→ ~ q	If not p, then not q. If it is not raining, you do not use an umbrella.
Contrapositive ~ q→ ~ p	If not q, then not p. If you are not using an umbrella, then it is not raining.

For problems 1–7, write the converse, inverse, and contrapositive statements based upon the given conditional statements.

1. If I own a horse, then I own an animal.
   Converse _____
   Inverse _____
   Contrapositive _____

2. If I study, then I do well in school.
   Converse _____
   Inverse _____
   Contrapositive _____

3. If today is Monday, then yesterday was Sunday.
   Converse _____
   Inverse _____
   Contrapositive _____

4. If it is Saturday, I do not go to school.
   Converse _____
   Inverse _____
   Contrapositive _____

5. If I do not go to bed early, I do not sleep well.
   Converse _____
   Inverse _____
   Contrapositive _____

6. If $6x = 18$, then $x = 3$.
   Converse _____
   Inverse _____
   Contrapositive _____

7. If $AB + BC = AC$, then B is between A and C.
   Converse _____
   Inverse _____
   Contrapositive _____

8. Given a conditional statement, the _____ statement is **always** true.
   (Choose from converse, inverse, or contrapositive.)

Logic Puzzle

Use the following statements to determine the names of the men playing each position on this baseball team.

1. Andy dislikes the catcher.
2. Ed's sister is engaged to the second basemen.
3. The center fielder is taller than the right fielder.
4. Harry and the third baseman live in the same building.
5. Paul and Allen each won $20.00 from the pitcher at pinochle.
6. Ed and the outfielders play poker during their free time.
7. The pitcher's wife is the third baseman's sister.
8. All the battery and infield, except Allen, Harry and Andy, are shorter than Sam. (battery = catcher and pitcher)
9. Paul, Andy, and the shortstop lost $150.00 each at the racetrack.
10. Paul, Harry, Bill, and the catcher took a trouncing from the second baseman at the pool.
11. Sam is undergoing divorce proceedings.
12. The catcher and the third baseman each have two children.
13. Ed, Paul, Jerry, the right fielder, and the center fielder are bachelors. The others are married.
14. The shortstop, the third baseman and Bill each cleaned up betting on the fight.
15. One of the outfielders is either Mike or Andy.
16. Jerry is taller than Bill. Mike is shorter than Bill. Each of them is heavier than the third baseman.

	C	P	SS	1st	2nd	3rd	LF	CF	RF
Mike									
Ed									
Harry									
Paul									
Allen									
Bill									
Jerry									
Sam									
Andy									

More Two-Column Proofs

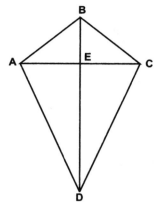

Complete the following proofs.

Given: $\overline{AB} \cong \overline{CB}$, $\overline{BD}$ bisects $\angle ABC$
Prove: $\overline{BD} \perp \overline{AC}$

Statements	Reasons
1. $\overline{AB} \cong \overline{CB}$, $\overline{BD}$ bisects $\angle ABC$	1. _____
2. $\angle ABE \cong \angle CBE$	2. _____
3. $\overline{BE} \cong \overline{BE}$	3. _____
4. $\triangle ABE \cong \triangle CBE$	4. _____
5. _____	5. CPCTC
6. _____	6. If 2 $\angle$s form a linear pair, they are supplementary.
7. $\angle BEA$ and $\angle BEC$ are right $\angle$s.	7. _____
8. $\overline{BD} \perp \overline{AC}$	8. _____

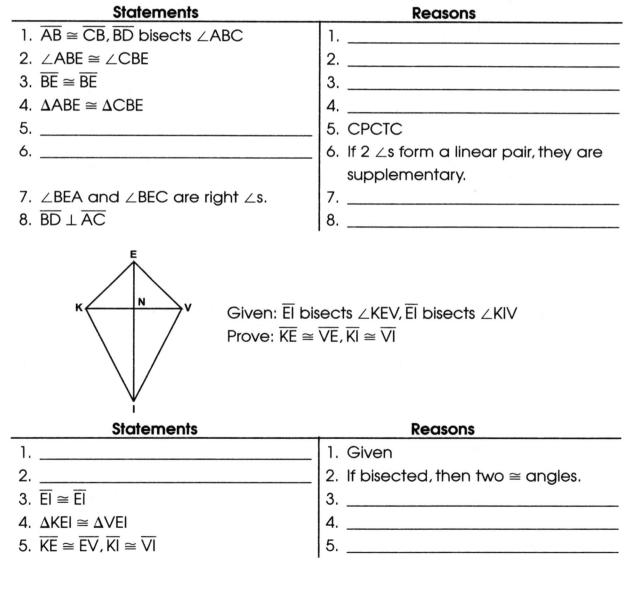

Given: $\overline{EI}$ bisects $\angle KEV$, $\overline{EI}$ bisects $\angle KIV$
Prove: $\overline{KE} \cong \overline{VE}$, $\overline{KI} \cong \overline{VI}$

Statements	Reasons
1. _____	1. Given
2. _____	2. If bisected, then two $\cong$ angles.
3. $\overline{EI} \cong \overline{EI}$	3. _____
4. $\triangle KEI \cong \triangle VEI$	4. _____
5. $\overline{KE} \cong \overline{EV}$, $\overline{KI} \cong \overline{VI}$	5. _____

More Two-Column Proofs

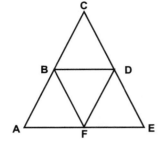

Given: B is the midpoint of $\overline{AC}$, D is the midpoint of $\overline{CE}$,
F is the midpoint of $\overline{AE}$

Prove: $\triangle CBD \cong \triangle BAF \cong \triangle DFE \cong \triangle FDB$

Statements	Reasons
1. _____	1. Given
2. $BF = \frac{1}{2} CE, BD = \frac{1}{2} AE, FD = \frac{1}{2} AC$	2. _____
3. _____	3. If midpoint, then two $\cong$ segments.
4. $AB = BC, AF = FE, CD = DE$	4. _____
5. _____	5. Definition of Between
6. $AB + AB = AC, CD + CD = CE,$ $AF + AF = AE$	6. _____
7. _____	7. Combining Similar Terms
8. $AB = \frac{1}{2} AC, CD = \frac{1}{2} CE, AF = \frac{1}{2} AE$	8. _____
9. _____	9. Substitution
10. $\overline{AB} \cong \overline{FD}, \overline{CD} \cong \overline{BF}, \overline{AF} \cong \overline{BD}$	10. _____
11. _____	11. Substitution
12. $\triangle CBD \cong \triangle BAF \cong \triangle DFE \cong \triangle FDB$	12. _____

How are the four small triangles and the one large triangle related?

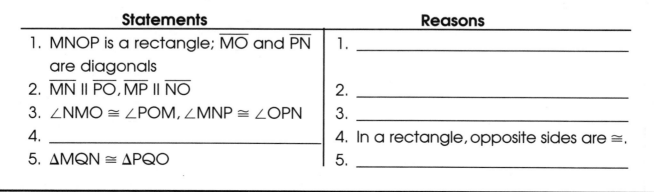

Given: MNOP is a rectangle; $\overline{MO}$ and $\overline{PN}$ are diagonals
Prove: $\triangle MQN \cong \triangle PQO$

Statements	Reasons
1. MNOP is a rectangle; $\overline{MO}$ and $\overline{PN}$ are diagonals	1. _____
2. $\overline{MN} \parallel \overline{PO}, \overline{MP} \parallel \overline{NO}$	2. _____
3. $\angle NMO \cong \angle POM, \angle MNP \cong \angle OPN$	3. _____
4. _____	4. In a rectangle, opposite sides are $\cong$.
5. $\triangle MQN \cong \triangle PQO$	5. _____

More Two-Column Proofs

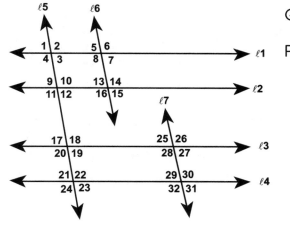

Given: $\angle 1 \cong \angle 7, \angle 1 \cong \angle 15, \angle 17 \cong \angle 27, \angle 17 \cong \angle 31,$
$\angle 9 \cong \angle 17$

Prove: $\ell_1 \parallel \ell_4$ and $\ell_5 \parallel \ell_7$

Statements	Reasons
1. _____	1. Given
2. $\ell_5 \parallel \ell_6$	2. _____
3. $\angle 7 \cong \angle 15$	3. _____
4. _____	4. If corresponding $\angle$s are $\cong$, then $\parallel$ lines.
5. _____	5. If corresponding $\angle$s are $\cong$, then $\parallel$ lines.
6. _____	6. Substitution
7. $\ell_3 \parallel \ell_4$	7. _____
8. $\ell_2 \parallel \ell_3$	8. _____
9. $\ell_1 \parallel \ell_3$	9. _____
10. $\ell_1 \parallel \ell_4$ and $\ell_5 \parallel \ell_7$	10. _____

Assume $\ell_1 \parallel \ell_2 \parallel \ell_3 \parallel \ell_4$ and $\ell_5 \parallel \ell_6 \parallel \ell_7$.

1. If $m\angle 9 = 70°$, then $m\angle 15 =$ _____.

2. If $m\angle 25 = 73°$, then $m\angle 22 =$ _____.

3. If $m\angle 18 = 120°$, then $m\angle 2 =$ _____.

4. If $m\angle 32 = 80°$, then $m\angle 12 =$ _____.

5. If $m\angle 3 = 84°$, then $m\angle 17 =$ _____.

6. If $m\angle 11 = 75°$, then $m\angle 23 =$ _____.

7. If $m\angle 28 = 100°$, then $m\angle 13 =$ _____.

8. If $m\angle 30 = 101°$, then $m\angle 19 =$ _____.

Radians

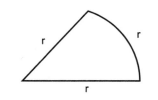

A **radian** is defined to be the measure of an angle which has its vertex at the center of a circle and which intercepts an arc whose length is equal to the radius.

The circumference and the radius are related by the equation C = 2π r.

Thus, there are 2π radians in the complete circle. From this, we can obtain the following:

$$2\pi \text{ radians} = 360°$$

$$1 \text{ radian} = \frac{180°}{\pi} = 57.3°$$

$$1° = \frac{\pi}{180°} \text{ radians} = 0.01745 \text{ radians}$$

Convert the following angle measures from degrees to radians or from radians to degrees.

$$\text{degrees} \times \frac{\pi}{180} = \text{radians} \qquad\qquad \text{radians} \times \frac{180}{\pi} = \text{degrees}$$

1. 180°

2. $\frac{\pi}{2}$ radians

3. 27°

4. 45°

5. 6.2832 radians

6. 4.7 radians

7. 2 radians

8. 90°

9. 0.05235 radians

10. $\frac{\pi}{3}$ radians

11. 1.0472 radians

12. 36°

Application of Radians

$$\theta \;=\; \frac{\pi}{2}\text{ rad., } r = 2 \qquad\qquad \theta \;=\; 45°, r = 8$$

$$S \;=\; \theta r \qquad\qquad\qquad\qquad\quad \theta \;=\; 45° \times \frac{\pi}{180°} = \frac{\pi}{4}\text{ radians}$$

$$\;=\; \left(\frac{\pi}{2}\right)(2) \qquad\qquad\quad\; S \;=\; \left(\frac{\pi}{4}\right)(8)$$

$$S \;=\; \pi \text{ units} \qquad\qquad\qquad S \;=\; 2\pi \text{ units}$$

The length of an arc is directly proportional to the size of the central angle. In other words, the greater the angle, the greater the arc. Since there are 2π radians in the complete circle, then the length of the arc can be expressed as $S = \theta r$, where θ is the measure of the central angle and S is the length of the arc.

Complete the following table.

	θ	r	S
1.	180°	1	
2.		1	3π
3.	$\frac{\pi}{4}$ rad.	5	
4.		2	4π
5.	2 rad.	3	
6.	$\frac{\pi}{2}$ rad.		2π
7.	45°	4	
8.	3 rad.		4
9.	1°	1	
10.	270°	6	

Polar Coordinates

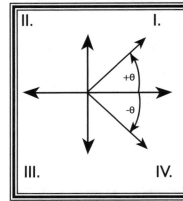

II.   I.   A point in a plane can also be given a unique representation by using polar coordinates. A positive angle is generated by the counterclockwise rotation of the positive x-axis about the origin. Similarly, a negative angle is generated by the clockwise rotation of the positive x-axis about the origin. A point can be named by giving the distance from the origin and the measure of the

III.   IV.   angle in the form (r, θ).

Graph the following polar coordinates.

1. $(2, \frac{\pi}{2})$

2. $(3, \pi)$

3. $(1, 45°)$

4. $(5, \frac{-\pi}{2})$

5. $(4, 270°)$

6. $(2, -\frac{3}{2}\pi)$

7. $(2, 540°)$

8. $(2, 2\pi)$

In which quadrant would you expect to find the following points?

9. $(2, \frac{\pi}{4})$

10. $(4, \frac{3}{4}\pi)$

11. $(3, \frac{-\pi}{3})$

12. $(1, \pi)$

13. $(2, \frac{15}{3}\pi)$

14. $(4, -\frac{4\pi}{3})$

15. $(3, ^-700°)$

16. $(^-1, 45°)$

Converting Polar and Rectangular Coordinates

The equations below can be used to convert between polar coordinates and rectangular coordinates.

$$x = r \cdot \cos \theta \qquad\qquad \tan \theta = \frac{y}{x}$$

$$y = r \cdot \sin \theta \qquad\qquad r = \sqrt{x^2 + y^2}$$

Find the polar coordinates corresponding to the following rectangular coordinates.

1. $(2, 0)$
2. $(3, 4)$

3. $(0, 5)$
4. $(4, 4)$

5. $(\bar{}2, \bar{}2)$
6. $(\bar{}6, 8)$

Find the rectangular coordinates corresponding to the following polar coordinates.

7. $(2, \frac{\pi}{2})$
8. $(3, \frac{-\pi}{4})$

9. $(4, \pi)$
10. $(2, 0)$

11. $(5, \frac{\pi}{3})$
12. $(\sqrt{2}, \frac{\pi}{4})$

Express the following equations in polar notation.

13. $x = 2$
16. $y = 4$

14. $x^2 + y^2 = 4$
17. $x^2 + y^2 - 3 = 13$

15. $y = 2x + 1$
18. $y = 3x$

Express the following equations in rectangular notation.

19. $r = 5$
22. $r = 2 \sec \theta$

20. $r = 3 \csc \theta$
23. $r = 7$

21. $\tan \theta = 3$
24. $\tan \theta = 2$

Graphs of Sine and Cosine Functions I

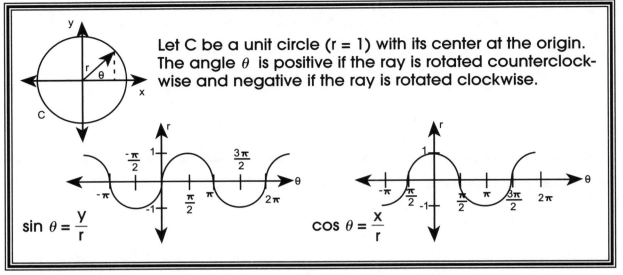

Let C be a unit circle (r = 1) with its center at the origin. The angle θ is positive if the ray is rotated counterclockwise and negative if the ray is rotated clockwise.

$$\sin \theta = \frac{y}{r}$$

$$\cos \theta = \frac{x}{r}$$

Complete the following table of values.

	y = sin x				y = cos x	
	x	**y**			**x**	**y**
1.	0	_____	7.		0	_____
2.	$\frac{\pi}{2}$	_____	8.		$\frac{\pi}{2}$	_____
3.	π	_____	9.		π	_____
4.	$\frac{3\pi}{2}$	_____	10.		$\frac{3\pi}{2}$	_____
5.	2π	_____	11.		2π	_____
6.	$\frac{-\pi}{2}$	_____	12.		$\frac{-\pi}{2}$	_____

13. What is the value of y when sin θ = 0?

14. At what values of θ is sin θ = 0?

15. What is the greatest value sin θ may assume?

16. Name two values of θ that make sin θ a maximum.

17. When is cos θ = 0?

18. What range of values may cos θ assume?

19. What is the value of sin θ when θ = 90°?

20. θ = π radian. What is sin θ? What is cos θ?

21. θ = ⁻4π radian. What is sin θ? What is cos θ?

22. θ = $\frac{3\pi}{2}$ radian cos θ = $\frac{x}{r}$ What is the value of x?

Graphs of Sine and Cosine Functions II

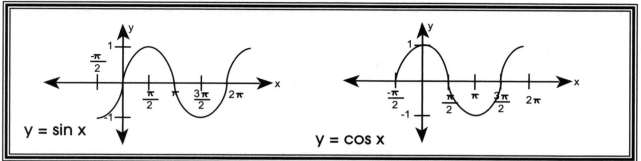

y = sin x   y = cos x

Consider the graph y = 2 sin x.

1. Where will it cross the x-axis?
2. Graph y = 2 sin x.
3. What is the range of y = 2 sin x?

In the equations y = a sin x and y = a cos x, |a| is called the **amplitude** of the curve.

4. What is the amplitude of y = 3 cos x?
5. Graph y = 3 cos x.
6. Where does y = 3 cos x cross the x-axis?
7. How does y = 3 cos x compare to y = cos x?

y = sin x and y = cos x range over the same values each time x runs through an interval of 2π units. The curve is said to be periodic and its period is 2π.

8. Graph y = sin 2x. (Include at least x = 0, x = $\frac{\pi}{4}$, x = $\frac{\pi}{2}$.)
9. Where does y = sin 2x cross the x-axis?
10. What is the period of y = sin 2x?

Some Useful Postulates and Theorems

Angle Addition Postulate (AAP) If a point X lies in the interior of $\angle ABC$, then $m\angle ABC = m\angle ABX + m\angle XBC$.

Supplement Postulate If two angles form a linear pair, then these two angles are supplementary.

Side-Angle-Side Postulate (SAS) If two sides and the included angle of one triangle are congruent to the corresponding parts of another triangle, then the two triangles are congruent.

Angle-Side-Angle Postulate (ASA) If two angles and the included side of one triangle are congruent to the corresponding parts of another triangle, then the two triangles are congruent.

Hypotenuse-Leg Postulate (HL) If the hypotenuse and one leg of a right triangle are congruent to the corresponding parts of another right triangle, then the two triangles are congruent.

Parallel Postulate Given a line *l* and a point *p* not on *l* there is exactly one line parallel to *l* through *p*.

Congruence Postulate Given two congruent triangles, the triangular regions they determine have the same area.

Angle-Angle Postulate (AA) If two angles of one triangle are congruent to the corresponding angles of another triangle, then the two angles are similar.

Area Addition Postulate If two or more polygonal regions intersect in only points, segments or not at all, then the area of their union is the sum of their individual areas.

Arc Addition Postulate If the arcs $\overparen{AC}$ and $\overparen{BC}$ of a circle intersect in the single point B, then $m\,\overparen{AB} + m\,\overparen{BC} = m\,\overparen{ABC}$.

Addition Property of Equality (APOE) If two sides of an equation are equal, then if an equal quantity is added to both sides the equation will still be equal.

Area	**Volume**
triangle $= \frac{1}{2} \cdot$ (base) $\cdot$ (height)	pyramid $= \frac{1}{3} \cdot$ (area of base) $\cdot$ (height)
rectangle $=$ (base) $\cdot$ (height)	cone $= \frac{1}{3} \cdot \pi \cdot$ (radius)$^2 \cdot$ (height)
square $=$ (side)^2	cylinder $= \pi \cdot$ (radius)$^2 \cdot$ (height)
parallelogram $=$ (base) $\cdot$ (height)	prism $=$ (area of base) $\cdot$ (height)
trapezoid $= \frac{1}{2} \cdot$ (height) $\cdot$ (sum of bases)	sphere $= \frac{4}{3} \cdot \pi \cdot$ (radius)^3
circle $= \pi \cdot$ (radius)^2	

Some Useful Definitions and Theorems

Between If A is on $\overline{BC}$, then A is between B and C if and only if $\overline{BA} + \overline{AC} = \overline{BC}$.

Bisect A bisects $\overline{BC}$ if A is the midpoint of $\overline{BC}$.

Complementary Angles Two angles are complementary if the sum of their measures is 90°.

CPCTC Corresponding parts of congruent triangles are congruent.

Midpoint A is the midpoint of $\overline{BC}$ if $\overline{BA} \cong \overline{AC}$.

Pythagorean Theorem $a^2 + b^2 = c^2$

Reflexive Property Given a segment, angle, triangle, etc. it is congruent to itself.

Right Angle A right angle is one that has a measure of 90°.

Right Triangle A right triangle is one that contains a right angle.

Substitution Given items a, b and c, if a = b and a = c, then b = c.

Supplementary Angles Two angles are supplementary if the sum of their measures is 180°.

Vertical Angles If the sides of two angles form opposite rays, then the angles are vertical angles.

- Vertical angles are congruent.
- If congruent, then equal.
- If equal, then congruent.
- Perpendicular lines form right angles.
- If parallel lines, then (corresponding, alternate interior, alternate exterior) angles are congruent.
- If parallel lines, then (same side interior, same side exterior) angles are supplementary.
- If (corresponding, alternate interior, alternate exterior) angles are congruent, then lines are parallel.
- If (same side interior, same side exterior) angles are supplementary, then the lines are parallel.
- Two lines parallel to a third are parallel.
- In a triangle, angles opposite congruent sides are congruent.
- In a triangle, sides opposite congruent angles are congruent.
- Complements of congruent angles are congruent.
- Supplements of congruent angles are congruent.
- The two acute angles of a right triangle are complementary.
- The sum of the angles of a triangle is 180°.
- In a triangle, if two angles are not congruent, then the larger side is opposite the larger angle.
- In a triangle, an exterior angle is greater than either remote interior angle.

Hinge Theorem: Given that two sides of one triangle are congruent to two sides of a second triangle and the included angle of the first triangle is smaller than the included angle of the second triangle, then the third side of the first triangle is smaller than the third side of the second triangle.

About the Authors

Mary Lee Vivian has helped numbers of secondary students master a variety of mathematical skills during her many years of teaching in the Parkway School District in St. Louis, Missouri. She holds a bachelor of arts degree in mathematics from Central Methodist College and a master's degree from the University of Missouri – St. Louis.

Tammy Bohn-Voepel is currently working on a Master of Science and a Doctor of Philosophy in Mathematics Degree at the University of Missouri. She holds a Bachelor of Science and a Bachelor of Arts degree in Mathematics and a Master of Arts in education, each from Northeast Missouri State University.

Margaret Thomas is currently a mathematics and science consultant for a major publisher. Her professional experience includes teaching mathematics grades seven through college in Ohio, California, Oklahoma, and Tennessee. For ten years, she served as the Mathematics-Science Coordinator K-12 for Putnam City Schools in Oklahoma City. Margaret is an active member of many professional organizations including NCTM. She currently lives in Indianapolis, Indiana.

Answer Key

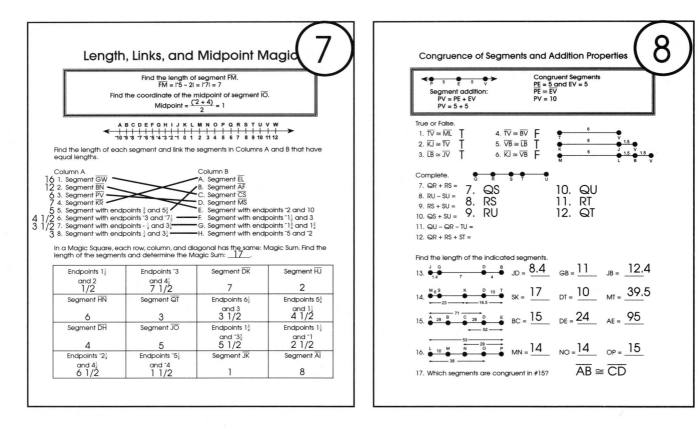

Answer Key

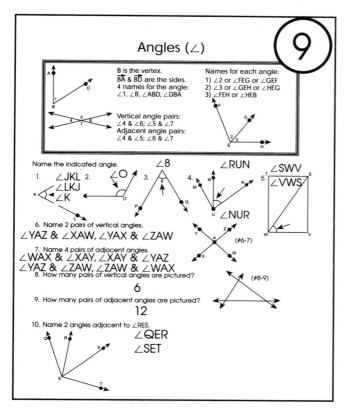

Angles (∠) ⑨

B is the vertex.
BA & BD are the sides.
4 names for the angle:
∠1, ∠B, ∠ABD, ∠DBA

Names for each angle:
1) ∠2 or ∠FEG or ∠GEF
2) ∠3 or ∠GEH or ∠HEG
3) ∠FEH or ∠HEB

Vertical angle pairs:
∠4 & ∠6; ∠5 & ∠7
Adjacent angle pairs:
∠4 & ∠5; ∠6 & ∠7

Name the indicated angle.

1. ∠JKL   ∠LKJ   ∠K   2. ∠O   3. ∠8   4. ∠RUN   ∠NUR   5. ∠SWV   ∠VWS

6. Name 2 pairs of vertical angles.
∠YAZ & ∠XAW, ∠YAX & ∠ZAW

7. Name 4 pairs of adjacent angles.
∠WAX & ∠XAY, ∠XAY & ∠YAZ
∠YAZ & ∠ZAW, ∠ZAW & ∠WAX   (#6-7)

8. How many pairs of vertical angles are pictured?
6   (#8-9)

9. How many pairs of adjacent angles are pictured?
12

10. Name 2 angles adjacent to ∠RES.
∠QER
∠SET

Congruence of Angles and Addition Properties ⑩

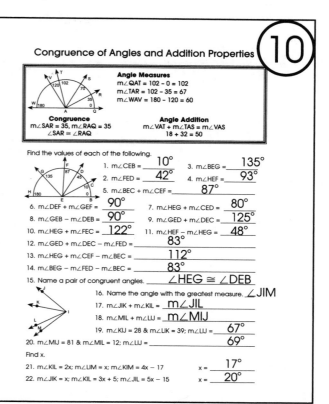

Angle Measures
m∠QAT = 102 − 0 = 102
m∠TAR = 102 − 35 = 67
m∠WAV = 180 − 120 = 60

Congruence
m∠SAR = 35, m∠RAQ = 35
∠SAR ≅ ∠RAQ

Angle Addition
m∠VAT + m∠TAS = m∠VAS
18 + 32 = 50

Find the values of each of the following.

1. m∠CEB = 10°   3. m∠BEG = 135°
2. m∠FED = 42°   4. m∠HEF = 93°
5. m∠BEC + m∠CEF = 87°
6. m∠DEF + m∠GEF = 90°   7. m∠HEG + m∠CED = 80°
8. m∠GEB − m∠DEB = 90°   9. m∠GED + m∠DEC = 125°
10. m∠HEG + m∠FEC = 122°   11. m∠HEF − m∠HEG = 48°
12. m∠GED + m∠DEC − m∠FED = 83°
13. m∠HEG + m∠CEF − m∠BEC = 112°
14. m∠BEG − m∠FED − m∠BEC = 83°
15. Name a pair of congruent angles. ∠HEG ≅ ∠DEB
16. Name the angle with the greatest measure. ∠JIM
17. m∠JIK + m∠KIL = m∠JIL
18. m∠MIL + m∠LIJ = m∠MIJ
19. m∠KIJ = 28 & m∠LIK = 39; m∠LIJ = 67°
20. m∠MIJ = 81 & m∠MIL = 12; m∠LIJ = 69°

Find x.
21. m∠KIL = 2x; m∠LIM = x; m∠KIM = 4x − 17   x = 17°
22. m∠JIK = x; m∠KIL = 3x + 5; m∠JIL = 5x − 15   x = 20°

Classifying Angles ⑪

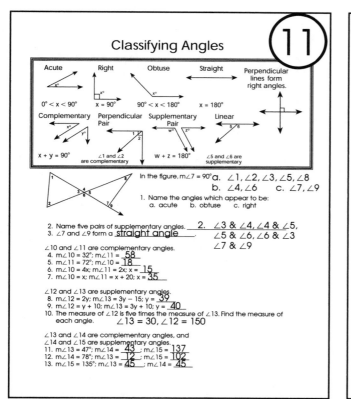

Acute   Right   Obtuse   Straight   Perpendicular lines form right angles.
0° < x < 90°   x = 90°   90° < x < 180°   x = 180°

Complementary   Perpendicular Pair   Supplementary Pair   Linear
x + y = 90°   ∠1 and ∠2 are complementary   w + z = 180°   ∠5 and ∠6 are supplementary

In the figure, m∠7 = 90°
a. ∠1, ∠2, ∠3, ∠5, ∠8
b. ∠4, ∠6   c. ∠7, ∠9

1. Name the angles which appear to be:
a. acute   b. obtuse   c. right

2. Name five pairs of supplementary angles.   2. ∠3 & ∠4, ∠4 & ∠5,
3. ∠7 and ∠9 form a **straight angle**.   ∠5 & ∠6, ∠6 & ∠3
∠7 & ∠9

∠10 and ∠11 are complementary angles.
4. m∠10 = 32°; m∠11 = 58
5. m∠11 = 72°; m∠10 = 18
6. m∠10 = 4x; m∠11 = 2x; x = 15
7. m∠10 = x; m∠11 = x + 20; x = 35

∠12 and ∠13 are supplementary angles.
8. m∠12 = 2y; m∠13 = 3y − 15; y = 39
9. m∠12 = y + 10; m∠13 = 3y + 10; y = 40
10. The measure of ∠12 is five times the measure of ∠13. Find the measure of each angle. ∠13 = 30, ∠12 = 150

∠13 and ∠14 are complementary angles, and ∠14 and ∠15 are supplementary angles.
11. m∠13 = 47°; m∠14 = 43; m∠15 = 137
12. m∠14 = 78°; m∠13 = 12; m∠15 = 102
13. m∠15 = 135°; m∠13 = 45; m∠14 = 45

Mixed Practice with Angles ⑫

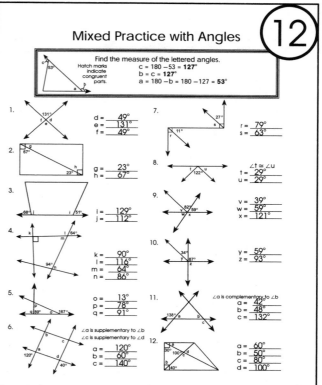

Find the measure of the lettered angles.
Hatch marks indicate congruent parts.
c = 180 − 53 = **127°**
b = c = **127°**
a = 180 − b = 180 − 127 = **53°**

1. d = 49°   e = 131°   f = 49°
2. g = 23°   h = 67°
3. i = 129°   j = 112°
4. k = 90°   l = 116°   m = 64°   n = 86°
5. o = 13°   p = 78°   q = 91°
6. ∠a is supplementary to ∠b   ∠c is supplementary to ∠b
a = 120°   b = 60°   c = 140°
7. r = 79°   s = 63°
8. ∠t ≅ ∠u   t = 29°   u = 29°
9. v = 39°   w = 59°   x = 121°
10. y = 59°   z = 93°
11. ∠a is complementary to ∠b   a = 42°   b = 48°   c = 132°
12. a = 60°   b = 50°   c = 80°   d = 100°

Answer Key

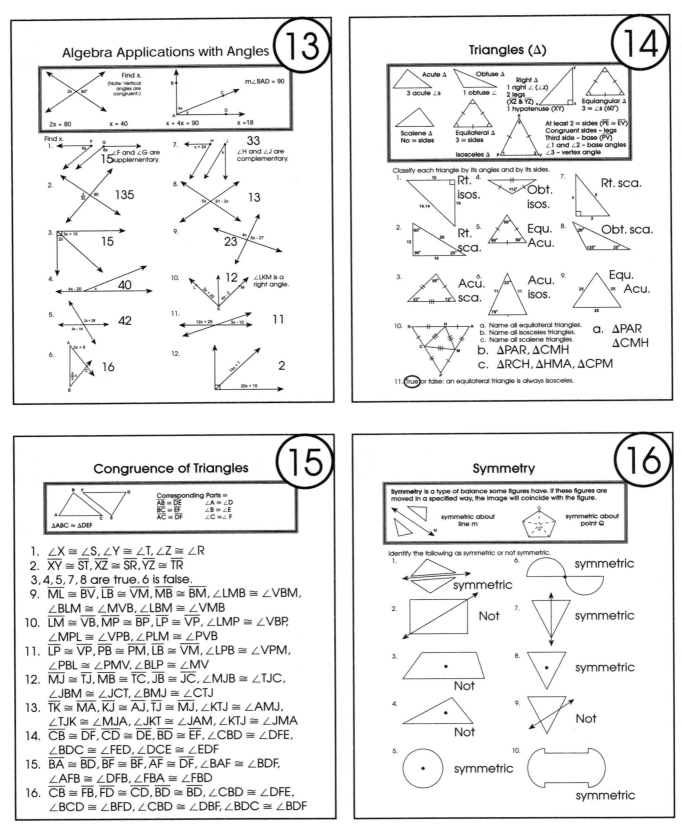

⑬ Algebra Applications with Angles

Find x.
(Note: Vertical angles are congruent.)

$2x = 80$ $x = 40$ $x + 4x = 90$ $x = 18$

m∠BAD = 90

Find x.

1. ∠F and ∠G are supplementary. **15**
2. **135**
3. **15**
4. **40**
5. **42**
6. **16**

7. ∠H and ∠J are complementary. **33**
8. **13**
9. **23**
10. ∠LKM is a right angle. **12**
11. **11**
12. **2**

⑭ Triangles (Δ)

Acute Δ — 3 acute ∠s
Obtuse Δ — 1 obtuse ∠
Right Δ — 1 right ∠ (∠z), 2 legs (XZ & YZ), 1 hypotenuse (XY)
Equiangular Δ — 3 ≅ ∠s (60°)
Scalene Δ — No ≅ sides
Equilateral Δ — 3 ≅ sides
Isosceles Δ — At least 2 ≅ sides (PE ≅ EV), Congruent sides – legs, Third side – base (PV), ∠1 and ∠2 – base angles, ∠3 – vertex angle

Classify each triangle by its angles and by its sides.

1. Rt. isos.
2. Rt. sca.
3. Acu. sca.
4. Obt. isos.
5. Equ. Acu.
6. Acu. isos.
7. Rt. sca.
8. Obt. sca.
9. Equ. Acu.

10.
a. Name all equilateral triangles.
b. Name all isosceles triangles.
c. Name all scalene triangles.

a. ΔPAR, ΔCMH
b. ΔPAR, ΔCMH
c. ΔRCH, ΔHMA, ΔCPM

11. (True) or false: an equilateral triangle is always isosceles.

⑮ Congruence of Triangles

ΔABC ≅ ΔDEF

Corresponding Parts ≅
AB ≅ DE   ∠A ≅ ∠D
BC ≅ EF   ∠B ≅ ∠E
AC ≅ DF   ∠C ≅ ∠F

1. ∠X ≅ ∠S, ∠Y ≅ ∠T, ∠Z ≅ ∠R
2. XY ≅ ST, XZ ≅ SR, YZ ≅ TR
3, 4, 5, 7, 8 are true. 6 is false.
9. ML ≅ BV, LB ≅ VM, MB ≅ BM, ∠LMB ≅ ∠VBM, ∠BLM ≅ ∠MVB, ∠LBM ≅ ∠VMB
10. LM ≅ VB, MP ≅ BP, LP ≅ VP, ∠LMP ≅ ∠VBP, ∠MPL ≅ ∠VPB, ∠PLM ≅ ∠PVB
11. LP ≅ VP, PB ≅ PM, LB ≅ VM, ∠LPB ≅ ∠VPM, ∠PBL ≅ ∠PMV, ∠BLP ≅ ∠MV
12. MJ ≅ TJ, MB ≅ TC, JB ≅ JC, ∠MJB ≅ ∠TJC, ∠JBM ≅ ∠JCT, ∠BMJ ≅ ∠CTJ
13. TK ≅ MA, KJ ≅ AJ, TJ ≅ MJ, ∠KTJ ≅ ∠AMJ, ∠TJK ≅ ∠MJA, ∠JKT ≅ ∠JAM, ∠KTJ ≅ ∠JMA
14. CB ≅ DF, CD ≅ DE, BD ≅ EF, ∠CBD ≅ ∠DFE, ∠BDC ≅ ∠FED, ∠DCE ≅ ∠EDF
15. BA ≅ BD, BF ≅ BF, AF ≅ DF, ∠BAF ≅ ∠BDF, ∠AFB ≅ ∠DFB, ∠FBA ≅ ∠FBD
16. CB ≅ FB, FD ≅ CD, BD ≅ BD, ∠CBD ≅ ∠DFE, ∠BCD ≅ ∠BFD, ∠CBD ≅ ∠DBF, ∠BDC ≅ ∠BDF

⑯ Symmetry

Symmetry is a type of balance some figures have. If these figures are moved in a specified way, the image will coincide with the figure.

symmetric about line m

symmetric about point Q

Identify the following as symmetric or not symmetric.

1. symmetric
2. Not
3. Not
4. Not
5. symmetric

6. symmetric
7. symmetric
8. symmetric
9. Not
10. symmetric

0-7424-1776-X *Geometry*

Answer Key

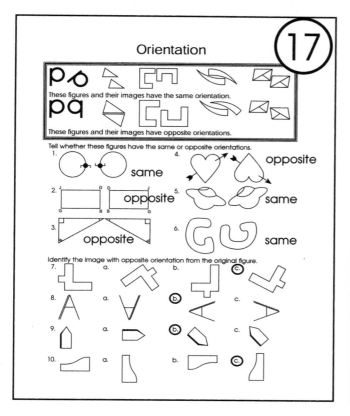

Orientation ⑰

These figures and their images have the same orientation.

These figures and their images have opposite orientations.

Tell whether these figures have the same or opposite orientations.

1. same
2. opposite
3. opposite
4. opposite
5. same
6. same

Identify the image with opposite orientation from the original figure.

7. ⓒ
8. ⓑ
9. ⓑ
10. ⓒ

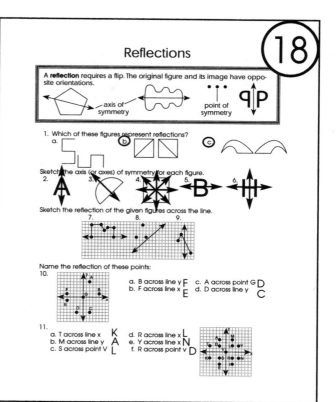

Reflections ⑱

A **reflection** requires a flip. The original figure and its image have opposite orientations.

axis of symmetry
point of symmetry

1. Which of these figures represent reflections?
   ⓑ ⓒ

Sketch the axis (or axes) of symmetry for each figure.
2. 3. 4. 5. 6.

Sketch the reflection of the given figures across the line.
7. 8. 9.

Name the reflection of these points:
10.
   a. B across line y — F
   b. F across line x — E
   c. A across point G — D
   d. D across line y — C

11.
   a. T across line x — K
   b. M across line y — A
   c. S across point V — L
   d. R across line x — L
   e. Y across line x — N
   f. R across point v — D

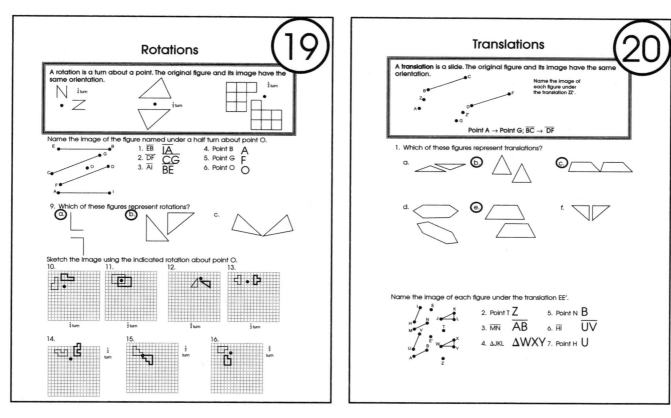

Rotations ⑲

A rotation is a turn about a point. The original figure and its image have the same orientation.

N ¼ turn
Z
½ turn
¾ turn

Name the image of the figure named under a half turn about point O.
1. EB — IA
2. DF — CG
3. AI — BE
4. Point B — A
5. Point G — F
6. Point O — O

9. Which of these figures represent rotations?
   ⓐ ⓑ c.

Sketch the image using the indicated rotation about point O.
10. ¼ turn
11. ½ turn
12. ¾ turn
13. ¼ turn
14. ¼ turn
15. ½ turn
16. ¾ turn

Translations ⑳

A **translation** is a slide. The original figure and its image have the same orientation.

Name the image of each figure under the translation ZZ'.

Point A → Point G; BC → DF

1. Which of these figures represent translations?
   a. ⓑ ⓒ
   d. ⓔ f.

Name the image of each figure under the translation EE'.
2. Point T — Z
3. MN — AB
4. △JKL — △WXY
5. Point N — B
6. HI — UV
7. Point H — U

0-7424-1776-X *Geometry*

Answer Key

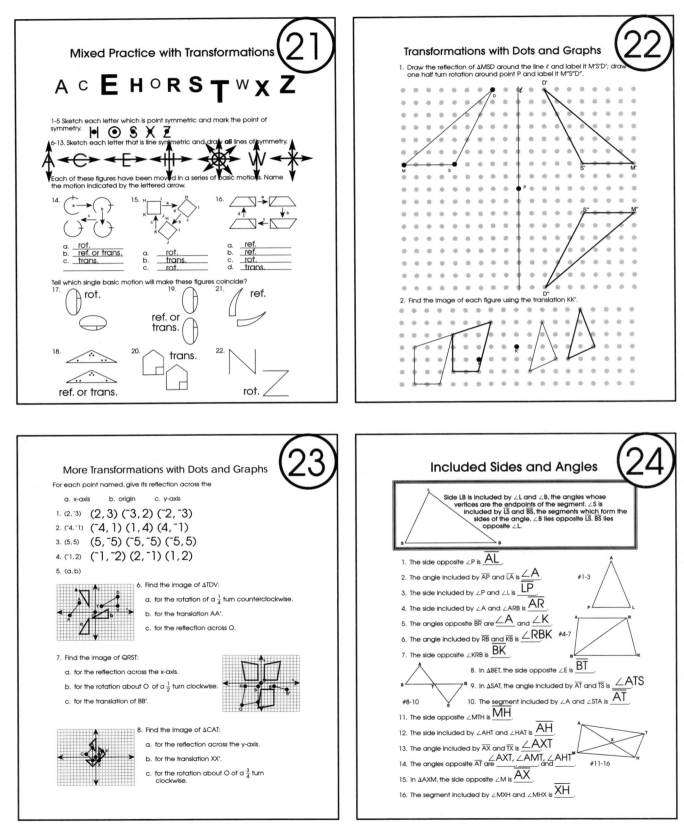

Mixed Practice with Transformations ㉑

A c **E** H o R S **T** w **X Z**

1-5 Sketch each letter which is point symmetric and mark the point of symmetry. H ⊙ S X Z

6-13. Sketch each letter that is line symmetric and draw **all** lines of symmetry. A C E H ✳ W X

Each of these figures have been moved in a series of basic motions. Name the motion indicated by the lettered arrow.

14.
a. rot.
b. ref. or trans.
c. trans.

15.
a. rot.
b. trans.
c. rot.

16.
a. ref.
b. ref.
c. rot.
d. trans.

Tell which single basic motion will make these figures coincide?

17. rot.

18. ref. or trans.

19. ref. or trans.

20. trans.

21. ref.

22. rot.

Transformations with Dots and Graphs ㉒

1. Draw the reflection of △MSD around the line ℓ and label it M'S'D'; draw one half turn rotation around point P and label it M"S"D".

2. Find the image of each figure using the translation KK'.

More Transformations with Dots and Graphs ㉓

For each point named, give its reflection across the

    a. x-axis   b. origin   c. y-axis

1. (2, ‾3) (2, 3) (‾3, 2) (‾2, ‾3)

2. (‾4, ‾1) (‾4, 1) (1, 4) (4, ‾1)

3. (5, 5) (5, ‾5) (‾5, ‾5) (‾5, 5)

4. (‾1, 2) (‾1, ‾2) (2, ‾1) (1, 2)

5. (a, b)

6. Find the image of △TDV:
   a. for the rotation of a $\frac{1}{4}$ turn counterclockwise.
   b. for the translation AA'.
   c. for the reflection across O.

7. Find the image of QRST:
   a. for the reflection across the x-axis.
   b. for the rotation about O of a $\frac{1}{2}$ turn clockwise.
   c. for the translation of BB'.

8. Find the image of △CAT:
   a. for the reflection across the y-axis.
   b. for the translation XX'.
   c. for the rotation about O of a $\frac{3}{4}$ turn clockwise.

Included Sides and Angles ㉔

Side LB is included by ∠L and ∠B, the angles whose vertices are the endpoints of the segment. ∠S is included by $\overline{LS}$ and $\overline{BS}$, the segments which form the sides of the angle. ∠B lies opposite $\overline{LS}$. $\overline{BS}$ lies opposite ∠L.

1. The side opposite ∠P is $\overline{AL}$.

2. The angle included by $\overline{AP}$ and $\overline{LA}$ is ∠A.   #1-3

3. The side included by ∠P and ∠L is $\overline{LP}$.

4. The side included by ∠A and ∠ARB is $\overline{AR}$.

5. The angles opposite $\overline{BR}$ are ∠A and ∠K.   #4-7

6. The angle included by $\overline{RB}$ and $\overline{KB}$ is ∠RBK.

7. The side opposite ∠KRB is $\overline{BK}$.

8. In △BET, the side opposite ∠E is $\overline{BT}$.

9. In △SAT, the angle included by $\overline{AT}$ and $\overline{TS}$ is ∠ATS.   #8-10

10. The segment included by ∠A and ∠STA is $\overline{AT}$.

11. The side opposite ∠MTH is $\overline{MH}$.

12. The side included by ∠AHT and ∠HAT is $\overline{AH}$.

13. The angle included by $\overline{AX}$ and $\overline{TX}$ is ∠AXT.

14. The angles opposite $\overline{AT}$ are ∠AXT, ∠AMT, and ∠AHT.   #11-16

15. In △AXM, the side opposite ∠M is $\overline{AX}$.

16. The segment included by ∠MXH and ∠MHX is $\overline{XH}$.

Answer Key

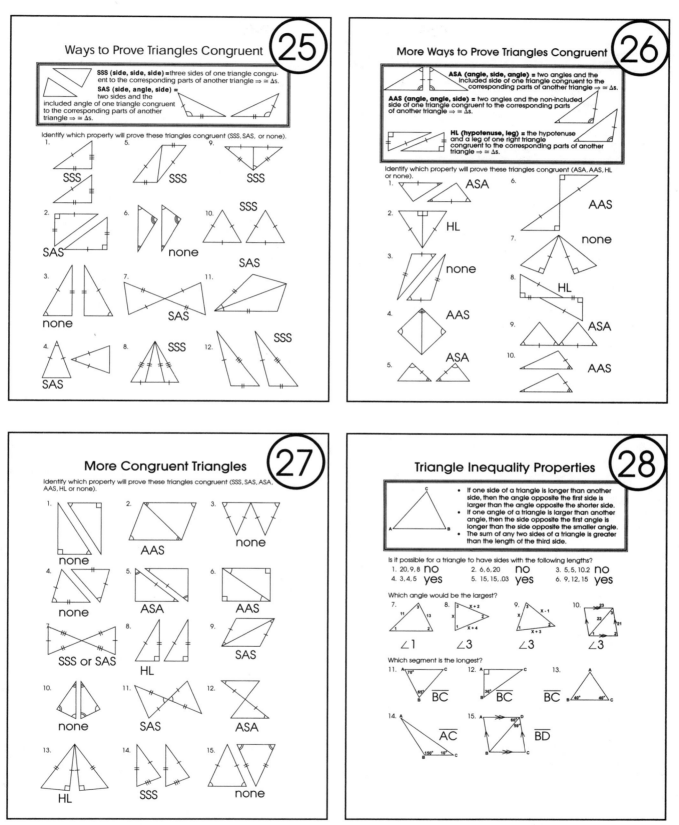

Ways to Prove Triangles Congruent (25)

SSS (side, side, side) = three sides of one triangle congruent to the corresponding parts of another triangle ⇒ ≅ Δs.

SAS (side, angle, side) = two sides and the included angle of one triangle congruent to the corresponding parts of another triangle ⇒ ≅ Δs.

Identify which property will prove these triangles congruent (SSS, SAS, or none).

1. SSS
2. SAS
3. none
4. SAS
5. SSS
6. none
7. SAS
8. SSS
9. SSS
10. SSS
11. SAS
12. SSS

More Ways to Prove Triangles Congruent (26)

ASA (angle, side, angle) = two angles and the included side of one triangle congruent to the corresponding parts of another triangle ⇒ ≅ Δs.

AAS (angle, angle, side) = two angles and the non-included side of one triangle congruent to the corresponding parts of another triangle ⇒ ≅ Δs.

HL (hypotenuse, leg) = the hypotenuse and a leg of one right triangle congruent to the corresponding parts of another triangle ⇒ ≅ Δs.

Identify which property will prove these triangles congruent (ASA, AAS, HL or none).

1. ASA
2. HL
3. none
4. AAS
5. ASA
6. AAS
7. none
8. HL
9. ASA
10. AAS

More Congruent Triangles (27)

Identify which property will prove these triangles congruent (SSS, SAS, ASA, AAS, HL or none).

1. none
2. AAS
3. none
4. none
5. ASA
6. AAS
7. SSS or SAS
8. HL
9. SAS
10. none
11. SAS
12. ASA
13. HL
14. SSS
15. none

Triangle Inequality Properties (28)

- If one side of a triangle is longer than another side, then the angle opposite the first side is larger than the angle opposite the shorter side.
- If one angle of a triangle is larger than another angle, then the side opposite the first angle is longer than the side opposite the smaller angle.
- The sum of any two sides of a triangle is greater than the length of the third side.

Is it possible for a triangle to have sides with the following lengths?

1. 20, 9, 8 no
2. 6, 6, 20 no
3. 5, 5, 10.2 no
4. 3, 4, 5 yes
5. 15, 15, .03 yes
6. 9, 12, 15 yes

Which angle would be the largest?

7. ∠1
8. ∠3
9. ∠3
10. ∠3

Which segment is the longest?

11. $\overline{BC}$
12. $\overline{BC}$
13. $\overline{BC}$
14. $\overline{AC}$
15. $\overline{BD}$

Answer Key

Proofs in Column Form (29)

Given: D is the midpoint of $\overline{AC}$ and $\overline{AB} \cong \overline{BC}$.
Prove: $\triangle ABD \cong \triangle CBD$.

Statements	Reasons
1. D is the midpoint of $\overline{AC}$	1. Given
2. $\overline{AD} \cong \overline{CD}$	2. Definition of Midpoint
3. $\overline{AB} \cong \overline{CB}$	3. Given
4. $\overline{BD} \cong \overline{BD}$	4. Reflexive Property
5. $\triangle ABD \cong \triangle CBD$	5. SSS

In each proof the Statements are in order but the Reasons are scrambled. Write the Reasons in the correct order.

Given: $\overline{GH}$ and $\overline{FJ}$ bisect each other.
Prove: $\triangle FGI \cong \triangle JHI$

Statements	Scrambled Reasons	Reasons
1. $\overline{GH}$ and $\overline{FJ}$ bisect each other.	1. Vertical angles are congruent.	2
2. $\overline{GI} \cong \overline{HI}$; $\overline{FI} \cong \overline{JI}$	2. Given	4
3. $\angle GIF \cong \angle HIJ$	3. SAS	1
4. $\triangle FGI \cong \triangle JHI$	4. Definition of Bisect	3

Given: KL = PO; LN = OM; KM = PN
Prove: $\triangle KLM \cong \triangle PON$

Statements	Scrambled Reasons	Reasons
1. LN = OM	1. Addition Property of Equality	2
2. LN + NM = NM + MO	2. Given	1
3. LN + NM = LM; NM + MO = NO	3. SSS	4
4. LM = NO	4. Definition of Between	6
5. KL = PO; KM = PN	5. Given	5
6. $\triangle KLM \cong \triangle PON$	6. Substitution Property	3

More Practice with Proofs (30)

Complete the following proofs.
Given: $m\angle 1 = 40°$; $m\angle 3 = 40°$, $\angle 2 \cong \angle 4$
Prove: $\triangle RTQ \cong \triangle TRS$

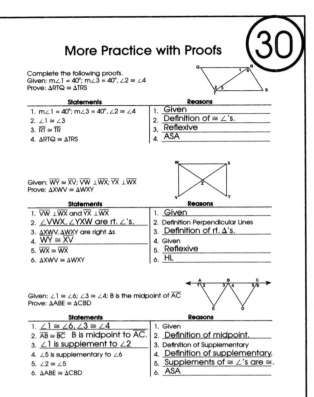

Statements	Reasons
1. $m\angle 1 = 40°$; $m\angle 3 = 40°$, $\angle 2 \cong \angle 4$	1. Given
2. $\angle 1 \cong \angle 3$	2. Definition of $\cong \angle$'s.
3. $\overline{RT} \cong \overline{TR}$	3. Reflexive
4. $\triangle RTQ \cong \triangle TRS$	4. ASA

Given: $\overline{WY} \cong \overline{XV}$; $\overline{VW} \perp \overline{WX}$; $\overline{YX} \perp \overline{WX}$
Prove: $\triangle XWV \cong \triangle WXY$

Statements	Reasons
1. $\overline{VW} \perp \overline{WX}$ and $\overline{YX} \perp \overline{WX}$	1. Given
2. $\angle VWX, \angle YXW$ are rt. $\angle$'s.	2. Definition Perpendicular Lines
3. $\triangle XWV, \triangle WXY$ are right $\triangle$s	3. Definition of rt. $\triangle$'s.
4. $\overline{WY} \cong \overline{XV}$	4. Given
5. $\overline{WX} \cong \overline{WX}$	5. Reflexive
6. $\triangle XWV \cong \triangle WXY$	6. HL

Given: $\angle 1 \cong \angle 6$; $\angle 3 \cong \angle 4$; B is the midpoint of $\overline{AC}$
Prove: $\triangle ABE \cong \triangle CBD$

Statements	Reasons
1. $\angle 1 \cong \angle 6$, $\angle 3 \cong \angle 4$	1. Given
2. $\overline{AB} \cong \overline{BC}$ B is midpoint to $\overline{AC}$.	2. Definition of midpoint.
3. $\angle 1$ is supplement to $\angle 2$	3. Definition of Supplementary
4. $\angle 5$ is supplementary to $\angle 6$	4. Definition of supplementary.
5. $\angle 2 \cong \angle 5$	5. Supplements of $\cong \angle$'s are $\cong$.
6. $\triangle ABE \cong \triangle CBD$	6. ASA

Fractal: Koch Curve (31)

In 1975, Benoit Mandelbrot used the term **fractal** to describe natural phenomena that appear to be chaotic, fragmented, and irregular but self-similar. Fractal designs can be created by iteration. An **iteration** is a repeated operation in which the output of one step becomes the input of the next. The starting object is called the **seed**.

Example: Draw a rectangle. Perform the iteration of connecting the midpoints of the adjacent sides. Every interior rectangle looks like the original—self-similar.

On another sheet of paper, complete Steps 0-3 to begin the Koch Curve.
Step 0 Draw a line segment 6 inches long. Ex. Step 0 _____ Consider its length to be one unit.
Step 1 Draw an equilateral triangle whose base is the middle third of the line segment. Do not draw the base.
Step 2 Draw an equilateral triangle on each segment so the base (not drawn) of each triangle is the middle third of the corresponding segment.
Step 3 Repeat Step 2.

Complete the table

Step	Number of Segments	Length of 1 Segment	Total Length
0	1	1	1
1	4	$\frac{1}{3}$	4/3
2	16	1/9	16/9
3	64	1/27	64/27

1. Describe the pattern in each column.

A. Number of segments is 4 times greater or 4^s (s = step number).
B. Length of 1 segment is 1/3 as much or $(1/3)^s$ (s = step number).
C. Total length is the product of answers A and B or $4^s(1/3)^s$ or $(4/3)^s$ (s = step number).
2. What would the values be for Step 5? 1,024 segments, each 1/243 units long for a total length of 1,024/243.
Historical Comment: The curve is the basis for the Koch Snowflake designed by Helge von Koch in 1904. Step 0 starts with an equilateral triangle. Steps 1, 2, 3, etc., are the same.

The Coordinate Plane (32)

Each point is designated by two coordinates (x, y).
Point A (3, 5)

The quadrants of the plane are numbered counterclockwise as shown.

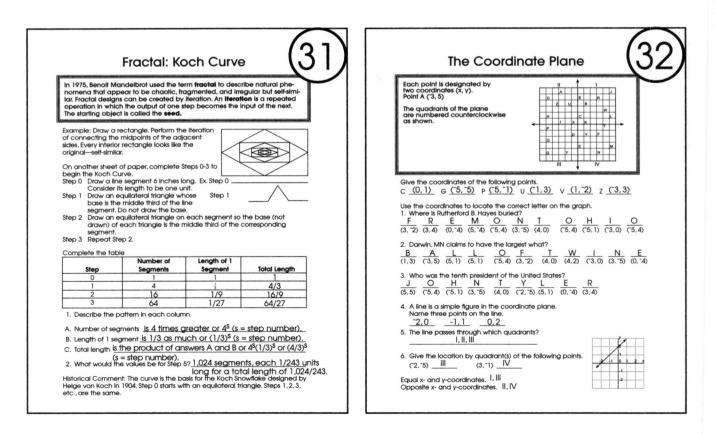

Give the coordinates of the following points.
C (0, 1) G (¯5, ¯5) P (5, ¯1) U (1, 3) V (1, ¯2) Z (¯3, 3)

Use the coordinates to locate the correct letter on the graph.
1. Where is Rutherford B. Hayes buried?
F R E M O N T   O H I O
(3, ¯2) (3, 4) (0, ¯4) (¯5, ¯4) (¯5, 4) (3, ¯5) (4, 0) (¯5, 4) (¯5, 1) (¯3, 0) (¯5, 4)

2. Darwin, MN claims to have the largest what?
B A L L   O F   T W I N E
(1, 3) (¯3, 5) (5, 1) (5, 1) (¯5, 4) (4, 0) (4, 2) (¯3, 0) (3, ¯5) (0, ¯4)

3. Who was the tenth president of the United States?
J O H N   T Y L E R
(5, 5) (¯5, 4) (¯5, 1) (3, ¯5) (4, 0) (¯2, ¯5) (5, 1) (0, ¯4) (3, 4)

4. A line is a simple figure in the coordinate plane.
Name three points on the line.
¯2, 0   -1, 1   0, 2

5. The line passes through which quadrants?
I, II, III

6. Give the location by quadrant(s) of the following points.
(¯2, ¯5) III   (3, ¯1) IV

Equal x- and y-coordinates. I, III
Opposite x- and y-coordinates. II, IV

0-7424-1776-X Geometry

Answer Key

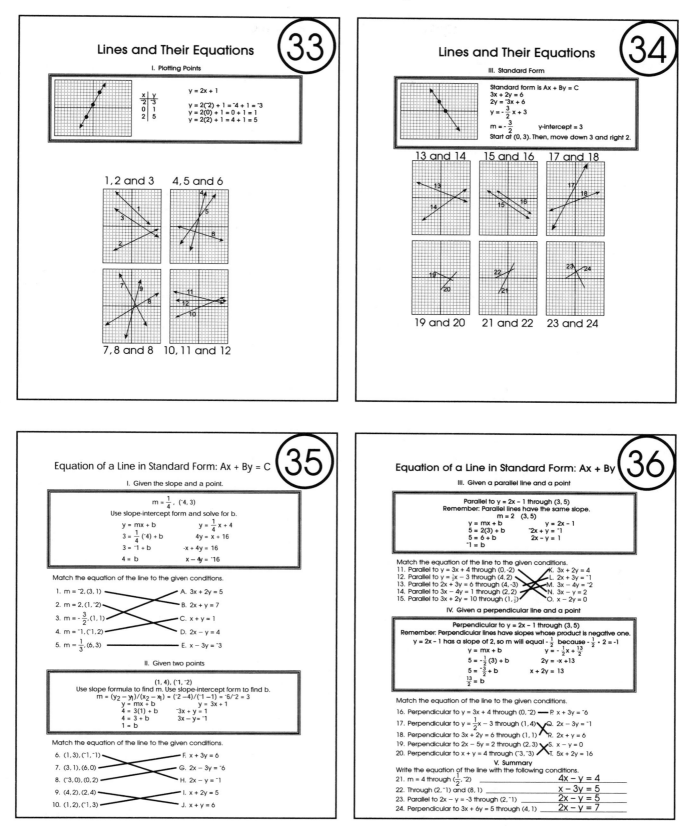

(33) Lines and Their Equations

I. Plotting Points

$y = 2x + 1$

x	y
‾2	‾3
0	1
2	5

$y = 2(‾2) + 1 = ‾4 + 1 = ‾3$
$y = 2(0) + 1 = 0 + 1 = 1$
$y = 2(2) + 1 = 4 + 1 = 5$

1, 2 and 3   4, 5 and 6

7, 8 and 8   10, 11 and 12

(34) Lines and Their Equations

III. Standard Form

Standard form is $Ax + By = C$
$3x + 2y = 6$
$2y = ‾3x + 6$
$y = -\frac{3}{2}x + 3$
$m = -\frac{3}{2}$ y-intercept = 3
Start at (0, 3). Then, move down 3 and right 2.

13 and 14   15 and 16   17 and 18

19 and 20   21 and 22   23 and 24

(35) Equation of a Line in Standard Form: Ax + By = C

I. Given the slope and a point.

$m = \frac{1}{4}$, (‾4, 3)
Use slope-intercept form and solve for b.

$y = mx + b$ $y = \frac{1}{4}x + 4$
$3 = \frac{1}{4}(‾4) + b$ $4y = x + 16$
$3 = ‾1 + b$ $-x + 4y = 16$
$4 = b$ $x - 4y = ‾16$

Match the equation of the line to the given conditions.

1. $m = ‾2, (3, 1)$ — A. $3x + 2y = 5$
2. $m = 2, (1, ‾2)$ — B. $2x + y = 7$
3. $m = -\frac{3}{2}, (1, 1)$ — C. $x + y = 1$
4. $m = ‾1, (‾1, 2)$ — D. $2x - y = 4$
5. $m = \frac{1}{3}, (6, 3)$ — E. $x - 3y = ‾3$

II. Given two points

(1, 4), (‾1, ‾2)
Use slope formula to find m. Use slope-intercept form to find b.
$m = (y_2 - y_1)/(x_2 - x_1) = (‾2 - 4)/(‾1 - 1) = ‾6/‾2 = 3$
$y = mx + b$ $y = 3x + 1$
$4 = 3(1) + b$ $‾3x + y = 1$
$4 = 3 + b$ $3x - y = ‾1$
$1 = b$

Match the equation of the line to the given conditions.

6. $(1, 3), (‾1, ‾1)$ — F. $x + 3y = 6$
7. $(3, 1), (6, 0)$ — G. $2x - 3y = ‾6$
8. $(‾3, 0), (0, 2)$ — H. $2x - y = ‾1$
9. $(4, 2), (2, 4)$ — I. $x + 2y = 5$
10. $(1, 2), (‾1, 3)$ — J. $x + y = 6$

(36) Equation of a Line in Standard Form: Ax + By

III. Given a parallel line and a point

Parallel to $y = 2x - 1$ through (3, 5)
Remember: Parallel lines have the same slope.
$m = 2$ (3, 5)
$y = mx + b$ $y = 2x - 1$
$5 = 2(3) + b$ $‾2x + y = ‾1$
$5 = 6 + b$ $2x - y = 1$
$‾1 = b$

Match the equation of the line to the given conditions.

11. Parallel to $y = 3x + 4$ through (0, ‾2) — K. $3x + 2y = 4$
12. Parallel to $y = \frac{1}{2}x - 3$ through (4, 2) — L. $2x + 3y = ‾1$
13. Parallel to $2x + 3y = 6$ through (4, ‾3) — M. $3x - 4y = ‾2$
14. Parallel to $3x - 4y = 1$ through (2, 2) — N. $3x - y = 2$
15. Parallel to $3x + 2y = 10$ through (1, ½) — O. $x - 2y = 0$

IV. Given a perpendicular line and a point

Perpendicular to $y = 2x - 1$ through (3, 5)
Remember: Perpendicular lines have slopes whose product is negative one.
$y = 2x - 1$ has a slope of 2, so m will equal $-\frac{1}{2}$ because $-\frac{1}{2} \cdot 2 = -1$
$y = mx + b$ $y = -\frac{1}{2}x + \frac{13}{2}$
$5 = -\frac{1}{2}(3) + b$ $2y = ‾x + 13$
$5 = \frac{‾3}{2} + b$ $x + 2y = 13$
$\frac{13}{2} = b$

Match the equation of the line to the given conditions.

16. Perpendicular to $y = 3x + 4$ through (0, ‾2) — P. $x + 3y = ‾6$
17. Perpendicular to $y = \frac{1}{2}x - 3$ through (1, 4) — Q. $2x - 3y = ‾1$
18. Perpendicular to $3x + 2y = 6$ through (1, 1) — R. $2x + y = 6$
19. Perpendicular to $2x - 5y = 2$ through (2, 3) — S. $x - y = 0$
20. Perpendicular to $x + y = 4$ through (‾3, ‾3) — T. $5x + 2y = 16$

V. Summary
Write the equation of the line with the following conditions.

21. $m = 4$ through $(\frac{1}{2}, ‾2)$ ____ $4x - y = 4$
22. Through (2, ‾1) and (8, 1) ____ $x - 3y = 5$
23. Parallel to $2x - y = ‾3$ through (2, ‾1) ____ $2x - y = 5$
24. Perpendicular to $3x + 6y = 5$ through (4, 1) ____ $2x - y = 7$

Answer Key

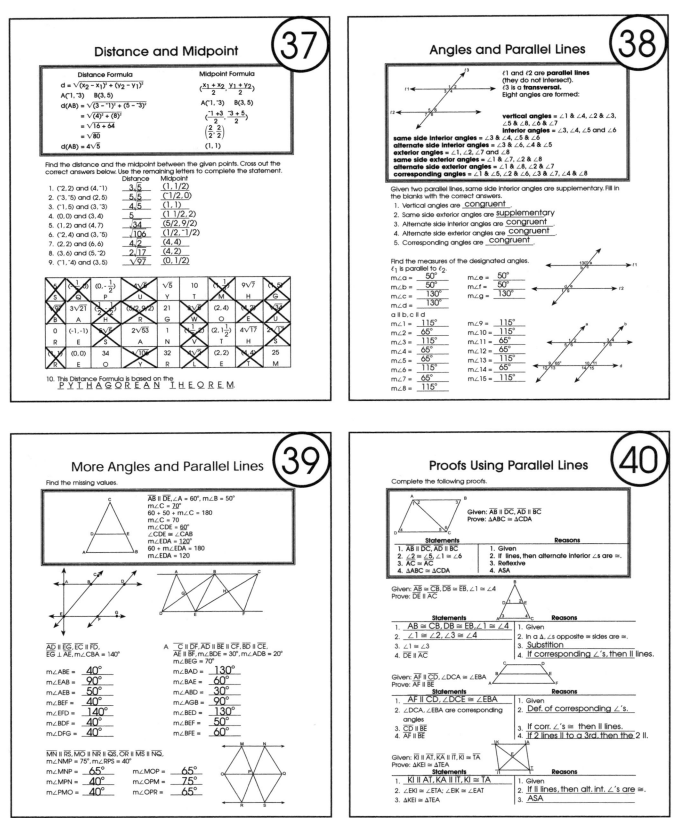

Distance and Midpoint (37)

Distance Formula	Midpoint Formula
$d = \sqrt{(x_2 - x_1)^2 + (y_2 - y_1)^2}$	$\left(\dfrac{x_1 + x_2}{2}, \dfrac{y_1 + y_2}{2}\right)$
A(⁻1, ⁻3) B(3, 5)	A(⁻1, ⁻3) B(3, 5)
$d(AB) = \sqrt{(3 - ^{-}1)^2 + (5 - ^{-}3)^2}$	$\left(\dfrac{^{-}1 + 3}{2}, \dfrac{^{-}3 + 5}{2}\right)$
$= \sqrt{(4)^2 + (8)^2}$	$\left(\dfrac{2}{2}, \dfrac{2}{2}\right)$
$= \sqrt{16 + 64}$	(1, 1)
$= \sqrt{80}$	
$d(AB) = 4\sqrt{5}$	

Find the distance and the midpoint between the given points. Cross out the correct answers below. Use the remaining letters to complete the statement.

		Distance	Midpoint
1.	(⁻2, 2) and (4, ⁻1)	3√5	(1, 1/2)
2.	(⁻3, ⁻5) and (2, 5)	5√5	(⁻1/2, 0)
3.	(⁻1, 5) and (3, ⁻3)	4√5	(1, 1)
4.	(0, 0) and (3, 4)	5	(1 1/2, 2)
5.	(1, 2) and (4, 7)	√34	(5/2, 9/2)
6.	(⁻2, 4) and (3, ⁻5)	√106	(1/2, ⁻1/2)
7.	(2, 2) and (6, 6)	4√2	(4, 4)
8.	(3, 6) and (5, ⁻2)	2√17	(4, 2)
9.	(⁻1, ⁻4) and (3, 5)	√97	(0, 1/2)

(⁻1, 0) C	(0, ⁻1/2) P	√5 U	√5 Y	10 T	(1, 1/2) M	9√7 H	(1, 5) G
√67 B	3√21 A	H	(5/2, 9/2) R	21 G	(2, 4) W	(2, 4) O	E	U
0 R	(⁻1, ⁻1) E	5√5 S	2√53 A	1 N	(1, 1/2) V	(2, 1 1/2) T	4√17 H	2√34 S
(0, 0) E	Y	34 O	√106 R	32 L	4√2 E	(2, 2) T	(4, 4) E	25 M

10. This Distance Formula is based on the
P Y T H A G O R E A N   T H E O R E M.

Angles and Parallel Lines (38)

$\ell 1$ and $\ell 2$ are **parallel lines** (they do not intersect).
$\ell 3$ is a **transversal.**
Eight angles are formed:

vertical angles = $\angle 1$ & $\angle 4$, $\angle 2$ & $\angle 3$, $\angle 5$ & $\angle 8$, $\angle 6$ & $\angle 7$
interior angles = $\angle 3$, $\angle 4$, $\angle 5$ and $\angle 6$
same side interior angles = $\angle 3$ & $\angle 4$, $\angle 5$ & $\angle 6$
alternate side interior angles = $\angle 3$ & $\angle 6$, $\angle 4$ & $\angle 5$
exterior angles = $\angle 1$, $\angle 2$, $\angle 7$ and $\angle 8$
same side exterior angles = $\angle 1$ & $\angle 7$, $\angle 2$ & $\angle 8$
alternate side exterior angles = $\angle 1$ & $\angle 8$, $\angle 2$ & $\angle 7$
corresponding angles = $\angle 1$ & $\angle 5$, $\angle 2$ & $\angle 6$, $\angle 3$ & $\angle 7$, $\angle 4$ & $\angle 8$

Given two parallel lines, same side interior angles are supplementary. Fill in the blanks with the correct answers.
1. Vertical angles are __congruent__.
2. Same side exterior angles are __supplementary__.
3. Alternate side interior angles are __congruent__.
4. Alternate side exterior angles are __congruent__.
5. Corresponding angles are __congruent__.

Find the measures of the designated angles.
ℓ_1 is parallel to ℓ_2.

m∠a = __50°__	m∠e = __50°__
m∠b = __50°__	m∠f = __50°__
m∠c = __130°__	m∠g = __130°__
m∠d = __130°__	

a ∥ b, c ∥ d

m∠1 = __115°__	m∠9 = __115°__
m∠2 = __65°__	m∠10 = __115°__
m∠3 = __115°__	m∠11 = __65°__
m∠4 = __65°__	m∠12 = __65°__
m∠5 = __65°__	m∠13 = __115°__
m∠6 = __115°__	m∠14 = __65°__
m∠7 = __65°__	m∠15 = __115°__
m∠8 = __115°__	

More Angles and Parallel Lines (39)

Find the missing values.

$\overline{AB} \parallel \overline{DE}, \angle A = 60°, m\angle B = 50°$
m∠C = __70°__
60 + 50 + m∠C = 180
m∠C = 70
m∠CDE = __60°__
∠CDE ≅ ∠CAB
m∠EDA = __120°__
60 + m∠EDA = 180
m∠EDA = 120

$\overline{AD} \parallel \overline{EG}, \overline{EC} \parallel \overline{FD},$
$\overline{EG} \perp \overline{AE}, m\angle CBA = 140°$

m∠ABE = __40°__	
m∠EAB = __90°__	
m∠AEB = __50°__	
m∠BEF = __40°__	
m∠EFD = __140°__	
m∠BDF = __40°__	
m∠DFG = __40°__	

A $\overline{C} \parallel \overline{DF}, \overline{AD} \parallel \overline{BE} \parallel \overline{CF}, \overline{BD} \parallel \overline{CE},$
$\overline{AE} \parallel \overline{BF}, m\angle BDE = 30°, m\angle ADB = 20°$
m∠BEG = 70°

m∠BAD = __130°__	
m∠BAE = __60°__	
m∠ABD = __30°__	
m∠AGB = __90°__	
m∠BED = __130°__	
m∠BEF = __50°__	
m∠BFE = __60°__	

$\overline{MN} \parallel \overline{RS}, \overline{MO} \parallel \overline{NR} \parallel \overline{QS}, \overline{OR} \parallel \overline{MS} \parallel \overline{NQ},$
m∠NMP = 75°, m∠RPS = 40°

m∠MNP = __65°__	m∠MOP = __65°__
m∠MPN = __40°__	m∠OPM = __75°__
m∠PMO = __40°__	m∠OPR = __65°__

Proofs Using Parallel Lines (40)

Complete the following proofs.

Given: $\overline{AB} \parallel \overline{DC}, \overline{AD} \parallel \overline{BC}$
Prove: $\triangle ABC \cong \triangle CDA$

Statements	Reasons
1. AB ∥ DC, AD ∥ BC	1. Given
2. ∠2 ≅ ∠5, ∠1 ≅ ∠6	2. If ∥ lines, then alternate interior ∠s are ≅.
3. $\overline{AC} \cong \overline{AC}$	3. Reflexive
4. △ABC ≅ △CDA	4. ASA

Given: $\overline{AB} \cong \overline{CB}, \overline{DB} \cong \overline{EB}, \angle 1 \cong \angle 4$
Prove: $\overline{DE} \parallel \overline{AC}$

Statements	Reasons
1. AB ≅ CB, DB ≅ EB, ∠1 ≅ ∠4	1. Given
2. ∠1 ≅ ∠2, ∠3 ≅ ∠4	2. In a △, ∠s opposite ≅ sides are ≅.
3. ∠1 ≅ ∠3	3. Substition
4. $\overline{DE} \parallel \overline{AC}$	4. If corresponding ∠'s, then ∥ lines.

Given: $\overline{AF} \parallel \overline{CD}, \angle DCA \cong \angle EBA$
Prove: $\overline{AF} \parallel \overline{BE}$

Statements	Reasons
1. AF ∥ CD, ∠DCE ≅ ∠EBA	1. Given
2. ∠DCA, ∠EBA are corresponding angles	2. Def. of corresponding ∠'s.
3. $\overline{CD} \parallel \overline{BE}$	3. If corr. ∠'s ≅ then ∥ lines.
4. $\overline{AF} \parallel \overline{BE}$	4. If 2 lines ∥ to a 3rd, then the 2 ∥.

Given: $\overline{KI} \parallel \overline{AT}, \overline{KA} \parallel \overline{IT}, \overline{KI} \cong \overline{TA}$
Prove: $\triangle KEI \cong \triangle TEA$

Statements	Reasons
1. KI ∥ AT, KA ∥ IT, KI ≅ TA	1. Given
2. ∠EKI ≅ ∠ETA; ∠EIK ≅ ∠EAT	2. If ∥ lines, then alt. int. ∠'s are ≅.
3. △KEI ≅ △TEA	3. ASA

Answer Key

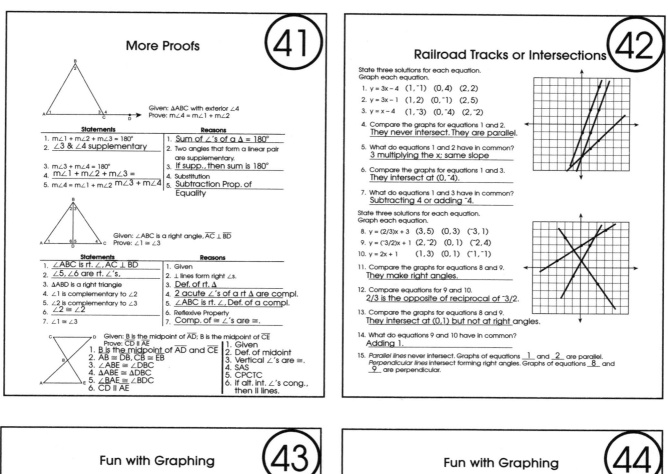

More Proofs (41)

Given: ΔABC with exterior ∠4
Prove: m∠4 = m∠1 + m∠2

Statements	Reasons
1. m∠1 + m∠2 + m∠3 = 180°	1. <u>Sum of ∠'s of a Δ = 180°</u>
2. ∠3 & ∠4 supplementary	2. Two angles that form a linear pair are supplementary.
3. m∠3 + m∠4 = 180°	3. <u>If supp., then sum is 180°</u>
4. <u>m∠1 + m∠2 + m∠3 =</u> <u>m∠3 + m∠4</u>	4. Substitution
5. m∠4 = m∠1 + m∠2	5. <u>Subtraction Prop. of Equality</u>

Given: ∠ABC is a right angle, $\overline{AC} \perp \overline{BD}$
Prove: ∠1 ≅ ∠3

Statements	Reasons
1. ∠ABC is rt. ∠, AC ⊥ BD	1. Given
2. ∠5, ∠6 are rt. ∠'s,	2. ⊥ lines form right ∠s.
3. ΔABD is a right triangle	3. <u>Def. of rt. Δ</u>
4. ∠1 is complementary to ∠2	4. <u>2 acute ∠'s of a rt Δ are compl.</u>
5. ∠2 is complementary to ∠3	5. <u>∠ABC is rt. ∠, Def. of a compl.</u>
6. <u>∠2 ≅ ∠2</u>	6. Reflexive Property
7. ∠1 ≅ ∠3	7. <u>Comp. of ∠'s are ≅.</u>

Given: B is the midpoint of $\overline{AD}$; B is the midpoint of $\overline{CE}$
Prove: $\overline{CD} \parallel \overline{AE}$

1. <u>B is the midpoint of $\overline{AD}$ and $\overline{CE}$</u>	1. Given
2. AB ≅ DB, CB ≅ EB	2. Def. of midpoint
3. ∠ABE ≅ ∠DBC	3. Vertical ∠'s are ≅.
4. ΔABE ≅ ΔDBC	4. SAS
5. ∠BAE ≅ ∠BDC	5. CPCTC
6. CD ∥ AE	6. If alt. int. ∠'s cong., then ∥ lines.

Railroad Tracks or Intersections (42)

State three solutions for each equation.
Graph each equation.

1. y = 3x – 4   (1, ⁻1)   (0, 4)   (2, 2)
2. y = 3x – 1   (1, 2)   (0, ⁻1)   (2, 5)
3. y = x – 4   (1, ⁻3)   (0, ⁻4)   (2, ⁻2)

4. Compare the graphs for equations 1 and 2.
   <u>They never intersect. They are parallel.</u>

5. What do equations 1 and 2 have in common?
   <u>3 multiplying the x; same slope</u>

6. Compare the graphs for equations 1 and 3.
   <u>They intersect at (0, ⁻4).</u>

7. What do equations 1 and 3 have in common?
   <u>Subtracting 4 or adding ⁻4.</u>

State three solutions for each equation.
Graph each equation.

8. y = (2/3)x + 3   (3, 5)   (0, 3)   (⁻3, 1)
9. y = (⁻3/2)x + 1   (2, ⁻2)   (0, 1)   (⁻2, 4)
10. y = 2x + 1   (1, 3)   (0, 1)   (⁻1, ⁻1)

11. Compare the graphs for equations 8 and 9.
    <u>They make right angles.</u>

12. Compare equations for 9 and 10.
    <u>2/3 is the opposite of reciprocal of ⁻3/2.</u>

13. Compare the graphs for equations 8 and 9.
    <u>They intersect at (0,1) but not at right angles.</u>

14. What do equations 9 and 10 have in common?
    <u>Adding 1.</u>

15. *Parallel lines* never intersect. Graphs of equations <u>1</u> and <u>2</u> are parallel.
    Perpendicular lines intersect forming right angles. Graphs of equations <u>8</u> and <u>9</u> are perpendicular.

Fun with Graphing (43)

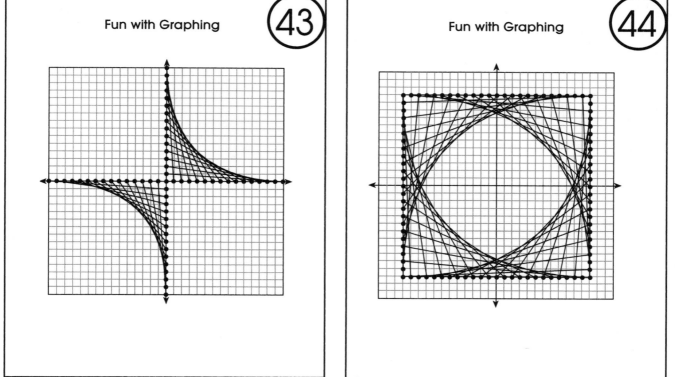

Fun with Graphing (44)

Answer Key

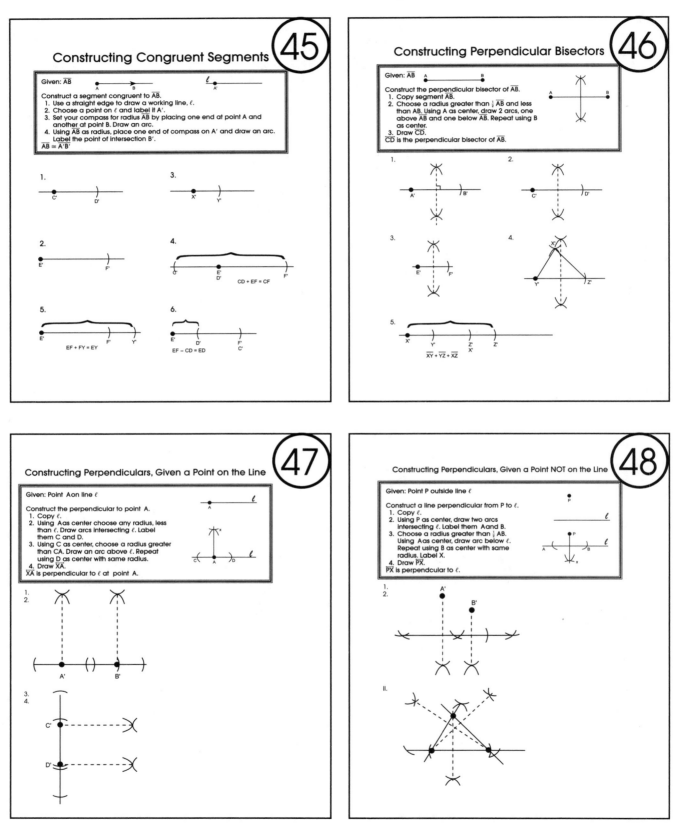

0-7424-1776-X *Geometry*

Answer Key

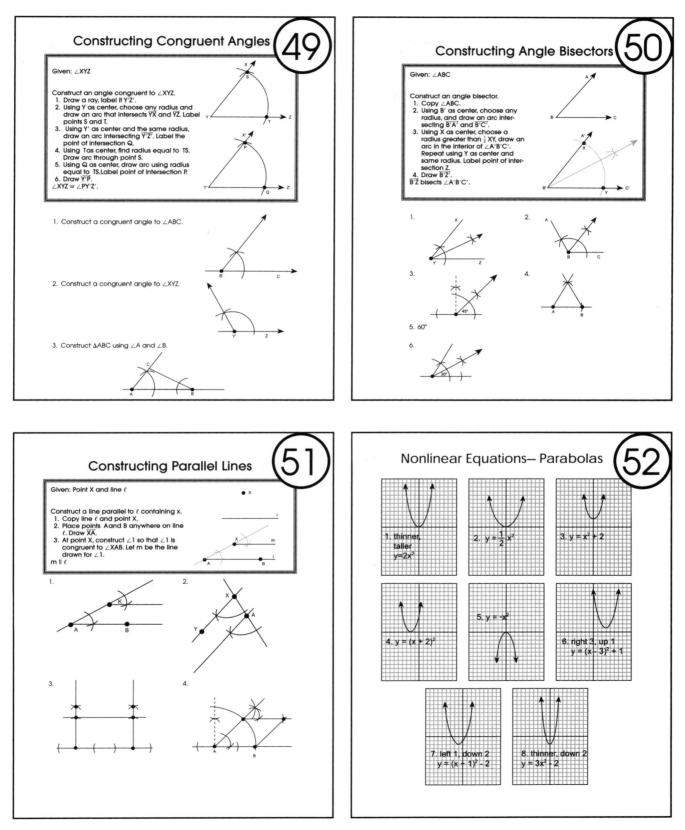

Constructing Congruent Angles — 49

Given: ∠XYZ

Construct an angle congruent to ∠XYZ.
1. Draw a ray, label it Y'Z'.
2. Using Y as center, choose any radius and draw an arc that intersects YX and YZ. Label points S and T.
3. Using Y' as center and the same radius, draw an arc intersecting Y'Z'. Label the point of intersection Q.
4. Using T as center, find radius equal to TS. Draw arc through point S.
5. Using Q as center, draw arc using radius equal to TS. Label point of intersection P.
6. Draw Y'P.
∠XYZ ≅ ∠PY'Z'.

1. Construct a congruent angle to ∠ABC.

2. Construct a congruent angle to ∠XYZ.

3. Construct ΔABC using ∠A and ∠B.

Constructing Angle Bisectors — 50

Given: ∠ABC

Construct an angle bisector.
1. Copy ∠ABC.
2. Using B' as center, choose any radius, and draw an arc intersecting B'A' and B'C'.
3. Using X as center, choose a radius greater than ½ XY, draw an arc in the interior of ∠A'B'C'. Repeat using Y as center and same radius. Label point of intersection Z.
4. Draw B'Z'.
B'Z bisects ∠A'B'C'.

1.

2.

3.

4.

5. 60°

6.

Constructing Parallel Lines — 51

Given: Point X and line ℓ

Construct a line parallel to ℓ containing x.
1. Copy line ℓ and point X.
2. Place points A and B anywhere on line ℓ. Draw XA.
3. At point X, construct ∠1 so that ∠1 is congruent to ∠XAB. Let m be the line drawn for ∠1.
m ‖ ℓ

1.

2.

3.

4.

Nonlinear Equations— Parabolas — 52

1. thinner, taller
y=2x²

2. y = ½x²

3. y = x² + 2

4. y = (x + 2)²

5. y = -x²

6. right 3, up 1
y = (x - 3)² + 1

7. left 1, down 2
y = (x - 1)² - 2

8. thinner, down 2
y = 3x² - 2

0-7424-1776-X Geometry

Answer Key

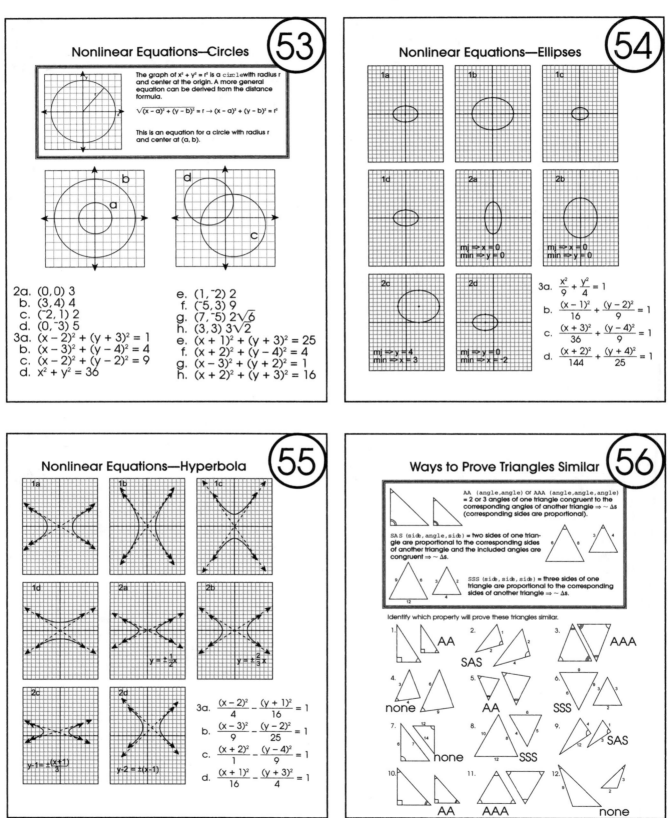

Nonlinear Equations—Circles (53)

The graph of $x^2 + y^2 = r^2$ is a circle with radius r and center at the origin. A more general equation can be derived from the distance formula.

$$\sqrt{(x-a)^2 + (y-b)^2} = r \to (x-a)^2 + (y-b)^2 = r^2$$

This is an equation for a circle with radius r and center at (a, b).

2a. (0,0) 3
 b. (3,4) 4
 c. (⁻2,1) 2
 d. (0,⁻3) 5
3a. $(x-2)^2 + (y+3)^2 = 1$
 b. $(x-3)^2 + (y-4)^2 = 4$
 c. $(x-2)^2 + (y-2)^2 = 9$
 d. $x^2 + y^2 = 36$

e. (1,⁻2) 2
f. (⁻5,3) 9
g. (7,⁻5) $2\sqrt{6}$
h. (3,3) $3\sqrt{2}$
e. $(x+1)^2 + (y+3)^2 = 25$
f. $(x+2)^2 + (y-4)^2 = 4$
g. $(x-3)^2 + (y+2)^2 = 1$
h. $(x+2)^2 + (y+3)^2 = 16$

Nonlinear Equations—Ellipses (54)

1a 1b 1c
1d 2a 2b

2a. mj ⇒ x = 0 / min ⇒ y = 0
2b. mj ⇒ x = 0 / min ⇒ y = 0

2c 2d

2c. mj ⇒ y = 4 / min ⇒ x = 3
2d. mj ⇒ y = 0 / min ⇒ x = ⁻2

3a. $\dfrac{x^2}{9} + \dfrac{y^2}{4} = 1$

b. $\dfrac{(x-1)^2}{16} + \dfrac{(y-2)^2}{9} = 1$

c. $\dfrac{(x+3)^2}{36} + \dfrac{(y-4)^2}{9} = 1$

d. $\dfrac{(x+2)^2}{144} + \dfrac{(y+4)^2}{25} = 1$

Nonlinear Equations—Hyperbola (55)

1a 1b 1c
1d 2a 2b

2a. $y = \pm\frac{1}{2}x$
2b. $y = \pm\frac{2}{3}x$

2c 2d

2c. $y-1 = \pm\frac{(x+1)}{3}$
2d. $y-2 = \pm(x-1)$

3a. $\dfrac{(x-2)^2}{4} - \dfrac{(y+1)^2}{16} = 1$

b. $\dfrac{(x-3)^2}{9} - \dfrac{(y-2)^2}{25} = 1$

c. $\dfrac{(x+2)^2}{1} - \dfrac{(y-4)^2}{9} = 1$

d. $\dfrac{(x+1)^2}{16} - \dfrac{(y+3)^2}{4} = 1$

Ways to Prove Triangles Similar (56)

AA (angle,angle) or AAA (angle,angle,angle) = 2 or 3 angles of one triangle congruent to the corresponding angles of another triangle ⇒ ~ Δs (corresponding sides are proportional).

SAS (side,angle,side) = two sides of one triangle are proportional to the corresponding sides of another triangle and the included angles are congruent ⇒ ~ Δs.

SSS (side,side,side) = three sides of one triangle are proportional to the corresponding sides of another triangle ⇒ ~ Δs.

Identify which property will prove these triangles similar.

1. AA
2. SAS
3. AAA
4. none
5. AA
6. SSS
7. none
8. SSS
9. SAS
10. AA
11. AAA
12. none

0-7424-1776-X *Geometry*

Answer Key

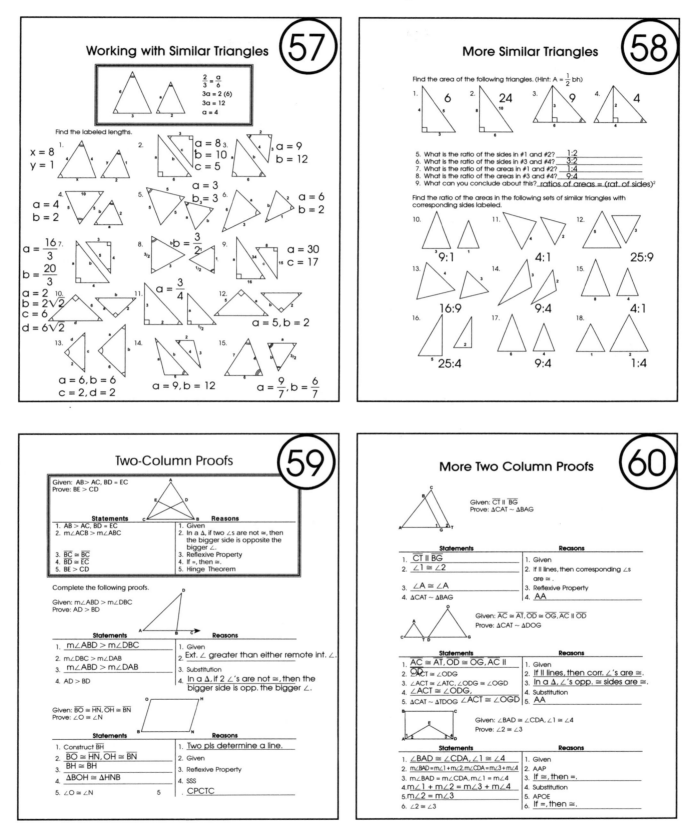

Working with Similar Triangles (57)

$$\frac{2}{3} = \frac{a}{6}$$
$3a = 2(6)$
$3a = 12$
$a = 4$

Find the labeled lengths.

1. $x = 8$, $y = 1$

2. $a = 8$, $b = 10$, $c = 5$

3. $a = 9$, $b = 12$

4. $a = 4$, $b = 2$

5. $a = 3$, $b = 3$

6. $a = 6$, $b = 2$

7. $a = \frac{16}{3}$, $b = \frac{20}{3}$

8. $b = \frac{3}{2}$

9. $a = 30$, $c = 17$

10. $a = 2$, $b = 2\sqrt{2}$, $c = 6$, $d = 6\sqrt{2}$

11. $a = \frac{3}{4}$

12. $a = 5$, $b = 2$

13. $a = 6$, $b = 6$, $c = 2$, $d = 2$

14. $a = 9$, $b = 12$

15. $a = \frac{9}{7}$, $b = \frac{6}{7}$

More Similar Triangles (58)

Find the area of the following triangles. (Hint: A = $\frac{1}{2}$ bh)

1. 6   2. 24   3. 9   4. 4

5. What is the ratio of the sides in #1 and #2? 1:2
6. What is the ratio of the sides in #3 and #4? 3:2
7. What is the ratio of the areas in #1 and #2? 1:4
8. What is the ratio of the areas in #3 and #4? 9:4
9. What can you conclude about this? ratios of areas = (rat. of sides)²

Find the ratio of the areas in the following sets of similar triangles with corresponding sides labeled.

10. 9:1   11. 4:1   12. 25:9

13. 16:9   14. 9:4   15. 4:1

16. 25:4   17. 9:4   18. 1:4

Two-Column Proofs (59)

Given: AB > AC, BD = EC
Prove: BE > CD

Statements	Reasons
1. AB > AC, BD = EC	1. Given
2. m∠ACB > m∠ABC	2. In a Δ, if two ∠s are not ≅, then the bigger side is opposite the bigger ∠.
3. $\overline{BC} \cong \overline{BC}$	3. Reflexive Property
4. $\overline{BD} \cong \overline{EC}$	4. If =, then ≅.
5. BE > CD	5. Hinge Theorem

Complete the following proofs.

Given: m∠ABD > m∠DBC
Prove: AD > BD

Statements	Reasons
1. m∠ABD > m∠DBC	1. Given
2. m∠DBC > m∠DAB	2. Ext. ∠ greater than either remote int. ∠.
3. m∠ABD > m∠DAB	3. Substitution
4. AD > BD	4. In a Δ, if 2 ∠'s are not ≅, then the bigger side is opp. the bigger ∠.

Given: $\overline{BO} \cong \overline{HN}$, $\overline{OH} \cong \overline{BN}$
Prove: ∠O ≅ ∠N

Statements	Reasons
1. Construct $\overline{BH}$	1. Two pts determine a line.
2. $\overline{BO} \cong \overline{HN}$, $\overline{OH} \cong \overline{BN}$	2. Given
3. $\overline{BH} \cong \overline{BH}$	3. Reflexive Property
4. ΔBOH ≅ ΔHNB	4. SSS
5. ∠O ≅ ∠N	5. CPCTC

More Two Column Proofs (60)

Given: $\overline{CT} \parallel \overline{BG}$
Prove: ΔCAT ~ ΔBAG

Statements	Reasons
1. $\overline{CT} \parallel \overline{BG}$	1. Given
2. ∠1 ≅ ∠2	2. If ∥ lines, then corresponding ∠s are ≅.
3. ∠A ≅ ∠A	3. Reflexive Property
4. ΔCAT ~ ΔBAG	4. AA

Given: $\overline{AC} \cong \overline{AT}$, $\overline{OD} \cong \overline{OG}$, $\overline{AC} \parallel \overline{OD}$
Prove: ΔCAT ~ ΔDOG

Statements	Reasons
1. $\overline{AC} \cong \overline{AT}$, $\overline{OD} \cong \overline{OG}$, AC ∥ OD	1. Given
2. ∠ACT ≅ ∠ODG	2. If ∥ lines, then corr. ∠'s are ≅.
3. ∠ACT ≅ ∠ATC, ∠ODG ≅ ∠OGD	3. In a Δ, ∠'s opp. ≅ sides are ≅.
4. ∠ACT ≅ ∠ODG, ∠ACT ≅ ∠OGD	4. Substitution
5. ΔCAT ~ ΔTDOG	5. AA

Given: ∠BAD ≅ ∠CDA, ∠1 ≅ ∠4
Prove: ∠2 ≅ ∠3

Statements	Reasons
1. ∠BAD ≅ ∠CDA, ∠1 ≅ ∠4	1. Given
2. m∠BAD = m∠1+m∠2, m∠CDA = m∠3+m∠4	2. AAP
3. m∠BAD = m∠CDA, m∠1 = m∠4	3. If ≅, then =.
4. m∠1 + m∠2 = m∠3 + m∠4	4. Substitution
5. m∠2 = m∠3	5. APOE
6. ∠2 ≅ ∠3	6. If =, then ≅.

Answer Key

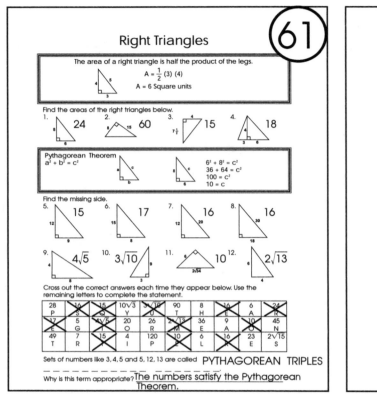

Right Triangles 61

The area of a right triangle is half the product of the legs.

$A = \frac{1}{2}$ (3) (4)

A = 6 Square units

Find the areas of the right triangles below.

1. 24 2. 60 3. 15 4. 18

Pythagorean Theorem

$a^2 + b^2 = c^2$

$6^2 + 8^2 = c^2$
$36 + 64 = c^2$
$100 = c^2$
$10 = c$

Find the missing side.

5. 15 6. 17 7. 16 8. 16
9. $4\sqrt{5}$ 10. $3\sqrt{10}$ 11. 10 12. $2\sqrt{13}$

Cross out the correct answers each time they appear below. Use the remaining letters to complete the statement.

28 P	16 ⊠	15 Y	10√3 U	3√10 ⊠	90 T	8 H	16 ⊠	6 A	24 R
17 E	5 G	4√5 ⊠	20 O	26 R	2√13 ⊠	36 M	9 E	10 A	45 O
49 T	7 R	⊠ 15	4 I	120 P	10 ⊠	6 L	⊠	23 E	2√15 S

Sets of numbers like 3, 4, 5 and 5, 12, 13 are called PYTHAGOREAN TRIPLES

Why is this term appropriate? The numbers satisfy the Pythagorean Theorem.

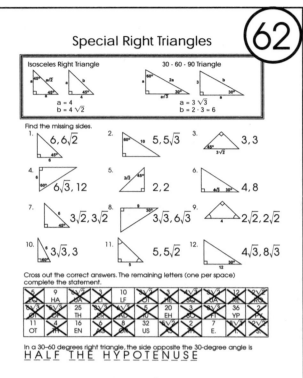

Special Right Triangles 62

Isosceles Right Triangle

a = 4
b = 4√2

30 - 60 - 90 Triangle

a = 3√3
b = 2 · 3 = 6

Find the missing sides.

1. $6, 6\sqrt{2}$ 2. $5, 5\sqrt{3}$ 3. $3, 3$
4. $6\sqrt{3}, 12$ 5. $2, 2$ 6. $4, 8$
7. $3\sqrt{2}, 3\sqrt{2}$ 8. $3\sqrt{3}, 6\sqrt{3}$ 9. $2\sqrt{2}, 2\sqrt{2}$
10. $3\sqrt{3}, 3$ 11. $5, 5\sqrt{2}$ 12. $4\sqrt{3}, 8\sqrt{3}$

Cross out the correct answers. The remaining letters (one per space) complete the statement.

In a 30–60 degrees right triangle, the side opposite the 30-degree angle is HALF THE HYPOTENUSE

Right Triangle Trigonometry 63

sine	$\sin \theta = \dfrac{\text{opposite}}{\text{hypotenuse}}$	$= \dfrac{a}{c}$
cosine	$\cos \theta = \dfrac{\text{adjacent}}{\text{hypotenuse}}$	$= \dfrac{b}{c}$
tangent	$\tan \theta = \dfrac{\text{opposite}}{\text{adjacent}}$	$= \dfrac{a}{b}$
cosecant	$\csc \theta = \dfrac{1}{\sin \theta}$	$= \dfrac{c}{a}$
secant	$\sec \theta = \dfrac{1}{\cos \theta}$	$= \dfrac{c}{b}$
cotangent	$\cot \theta = \dfrac{1}{\tan \theta}$	$= \dfrac{b}{a}$

	sin	cos	tan	csc	sec	cot
1.	3/5	4/5	3/4	5/3	5/4	4/3
2.	15/17	8/17	15/8	17/15	17/8	8/15
3.	7/25	24/25	7/24	25/7	25/24	24/7
4.	4/5	3/5	4/3	5/4	5/3	3/4
5.	4/5	3/5	4/3	5/4	5/3	3/4
6.	3/5	4/5	3/4	5/3	5/4	4/3
7.	√2/2	√2/2	1	√2	√2	1
8.	8/17	15/17	8/15	17/8	17/15	15/8
9.	8/17	15/17	8/15	17/8	17/15	15/8
10.	24/25	7/25	24/7	25/24	25/7	7/24
11.	√2/2	√2/2	1	√2	√2	1
12.	3√13/13	2√13/13	3/2	√13/3	√13/2	2/3

Solving Any Triangle 64

1. $\sin\theta\cos\theta - \cos\theta\sin\beta$
2. $\dfrac{\tan\theta + \tan\beta}{1 - \tan\theta \tan\beta}$
3. $\dfrac{\tan\theta - \tan\beta}{1 + \tan\theta\tan\beta}$
4. $-\sin\theta$

5. $-\cos\theta$
6. $\cos\theta$
7. $-\sin\theta$
8. $2\cos\theta\sin\theta$
9. $2\cos^2\theta - 1$
10. $\dfrac{2\cos\theta\sin\theta}{2\cos^2\theta - 1}$

1. $= 1 + \dfrac{\cos^2\theta}{\sin^2\theta}$

$= \dfrac{\sin^2\theta}{\sin^2\theta} + \dfrac{\cos^2\theta}{\cos^2\theta}$

$= \dfrac{1}{\sin^2\theta}$

$= \csc^2\theta$

2. $= 1 + \dfrac{\sin^2\theta}{\cos^2\theta}$

$= \dfrac{\cos^2\theta}{\cos^2\theta} + \dfrac{\sin^2\theta}{\cos^2\theta}$

$= \dfrac{1}{\cos^2\theta}$

$= \sec^2\theta$

3. $= \dfrac{1}{\cos\theta} - \dfrac{\sin\theta}{\cos\theta} \cdot \sin\theta$

$= \dfrac{1 - \sin^2\theta}{\cos\theta}$

$= \dfrac{\cos^2\theta}{\cos\theta}$

$= \cos\theta$

4. $= \dfrac{1}{\sin\theta} - \dfrac{\cos\theta}{\cos\theta} \cdot \sin\theta$

$= \dfrac{1 - \cos^2\theta}{\sin\theta}$

$= \dfrac{\sin^2\theta}{\sin\theta}$

$= \sin\theta$

0-7424-1776-X *Geometry*

Answer Key

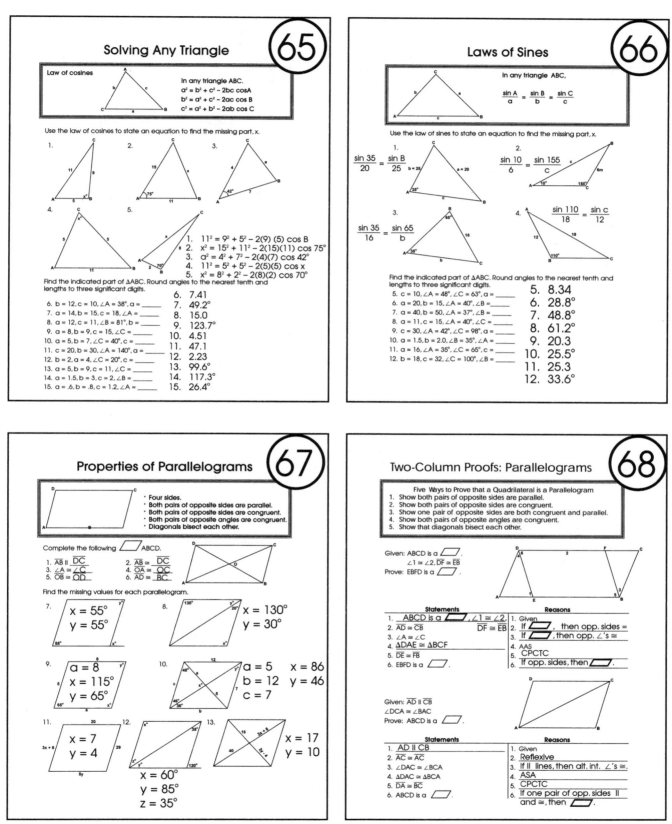

Solving Any Triangle (65)

Law of cosines

In any triangle ABC,
$a^2 = b^2 + c^2 - 2bc \cos A$
$b^2 = a^2 + c^2 - 2ac \cos B$
$c^2 = a^2 + b^2 - 2ab \cos C$

Use the law of cosines to state an equation to find the missing part, x.

1.   2.   3.

4.   5.

1. $11^2 = 9^2 + 5^2 - 2(9)(5) \cos B$
2. $x^2 = 15^2 + 11^2 - 2(15)(11) \cos 75°$
3. $a^2 = 4^2 + 7^2 - 2(4)(7) \cos 42°$
4. $11^2 = 5^2 + 5^2 - 2(5)(5) \cos x$
5. $x^2 = 8^2 + 2^2 - 2(8)(2) \cos 70°$

Find the indicated part of $\triangle ABC$. Round angles to the nearest tenth and lengths to three significant digits.

6. $b = 12, c = 10, \angle A = 38°, a = \_\_\_\_$
7. $a = 14, b = 15, c = 18, \angle A = \_\_\_\_$
8. $a = 12, c = 11, \angle B = 81°, b = \_\_\_\_$
9. $a = 8, b = 9, c = 15, \angle C = \_\_\_\_$
10. $a = 1.5, b = 7, \angle C = 40°, c = \_\_\_\_$
11. $c = 20, b = 30, \angle A = 140°, a = \_\_\_\_$
12. $b = 2, a = 4, \angle C = 20°, c = \_\_\_\_$
13. $a = 5, b = 9, c = 11, \angle C = \_\_\_\_$
14. $a = 1.5, b = 3, c = 2, \angle B = \_\_\_\_$
15. $a = .6, b = .8, c = 1.2, \angle A = \_\_\_\_$

6. 7.41
7. 49.2°
8. 15.0
9. 123.7°
10. 4.51
11. 47.1
12. 2.23
13. 99.6°
14. 117.3°
15. 26.4°

Laws of Sines (66)

In any triangle ABC,
$$\frac{\sin A}{a} = \frac{\sin B}{b} = \frac{\sin C}{c}$$

Use the law of sines to state an equation to find the missing part, x.

1. $\dfrac{\sin 35}{20} = \dfrac{\sin B}{25}$ 2. $\dfrac{\sin 10}{6} = \dfrac{\sin 155}{c}$

3. $\dfrac{\sin 35}{16} = \dfrac{\sin 65}{b}$ 4. $\dfrac{\sin 110}{18} = \dfrac{\sin c}{12}$

Find the indicated part of $\triangle ABC$. Round angles to the nearest tenth and lengths to three significant digits.

5. $c = 10, \angle A = 48°, \angle C = 63°, a = \_\_\_\_$
6. $a = 20, b = 15, \angle A = 40°, \angle B = \_\_\_\_$
7. $a = 40, b = 50, \angle A = 37°, \angle B = \_\_\_\_$
8. $a = 11, c = 15, \angle A = 40°, \angle C = \_\_\_\_$
9. $c = 30, \angle A = 42°, \angle C = 98°, a = \_\_\_\_$
10. $a = 1.5, b = 2.0, \angle B = 35°, \angle A = \_\_\_\_$
11. $a = 16, \angle A = 35°, \angle C = 65°, c = \_\_\_\_$
12. $b = 18, c = 32, \angle C = 100°, \angle B = \_\_\_\_$

5. 8.34
6. 28.8°
7. 48.8°
8. 61.2°
9. 20.3
10. 25.5°
11. 25.3
12. 33.6°

Properties of Parallelograms (67)

- Four sides.
- Both pairs of opposite sides are parallel.
- Both pairs of opposite sides are congruent.
- Both pairs of opposite angles are congruent.
- Diagonals bisect each other.

Complete the following $\diagdown$ ABCD.

1. $\overline{AB} \parallel \underline{DC}$
2. $\overline{AB} \cong \underline{DC}$
3. $\angle A \cong \underline{\angle C}$
4. $\overline{OA} \cong \underline{OC}$
5. $\overline{OB} \cong \underline{OD}$
6. $\overline{AD} \cong \underline{BC}$

Find the missing values for each parallelogram.

7. $x = 55°$ $y = 55°$
8. $x = 130°$ $y = 30°$
9. $a = 8$ $x = 115°$ $y = 65°$
10. $a = 5$ $b = 12$ $c = 7$ $x = 86$ $y = 46$
11. $x = 7$ $y = 4$
12. $x = 60°$ $y = 85°$ $z = 35°$
13. $x = 17$ $y = 10$

Two-Column Proofs: Parallelograms (68)

Five Ways to Prove that a Quadrilateral is a Parallelogram
1. Show both pairs of opposite sides are parallel.
2. Show both pairs of opposite sides are congruent.
3. Show one pair of opposite sides are both congruent and parallel.
4. Show both pairs of opposite angles are congruent.
5. Show that diagonals bisect each other.

Given: ABCD is a $\diagdown$.
$\angle 1 \cong \angle 2, \overline{DF} \cong \overline{EB}$
Prove: EBFD is a $\diagdown$.

Statements	Reasons
1. ABCD is a $\diagdown$, $\angle 1 \cong \angle 2$, $\overline{DF} \cong \overline{EB}$	1. Given
2. $\overline{AD} \cong \overline{CB}$	2. If $\diagdown$, then opp. sides =
3. $\angle A \cong \angle C$	3. If $\diagdown$, then opp. $\angle$'s $\cong$
4. $\triangle DAE \cong \triangle BCF$	4. AAS
5. $\overline{DE} \cong \overline{FB}$	5. CPCTC
6. EBFD is a $\diagdown$.	6. If opp. sides, then $\diagdown$.

Given: $\overline{AD} \parallel \overline{CB}$
$\angle DCA \cong \angle BAC$
Prove: ABCD is a $\diagdown$.

Statements	Reasons
1. AD $\parallel$ CB	1. Given
2. $\overline{AC} \cong \overline{AC}$	2. Reflexive
3. $\angle DAC \cong \angle BCA$	3. If $\parallel$ lines, then alt. int. $\angle$'s $\cong$.
4. $\triangle DAC \cong \triangle BCA$	4. ASA
5. $\overline{DA} \cong \overline{BC}$	5. CPCTC
6. ABCD is a $\diagdown$.	6. If one pair of opp. sides $\parallel$ and $\cong$, then $\diagdown$.

Answer Key

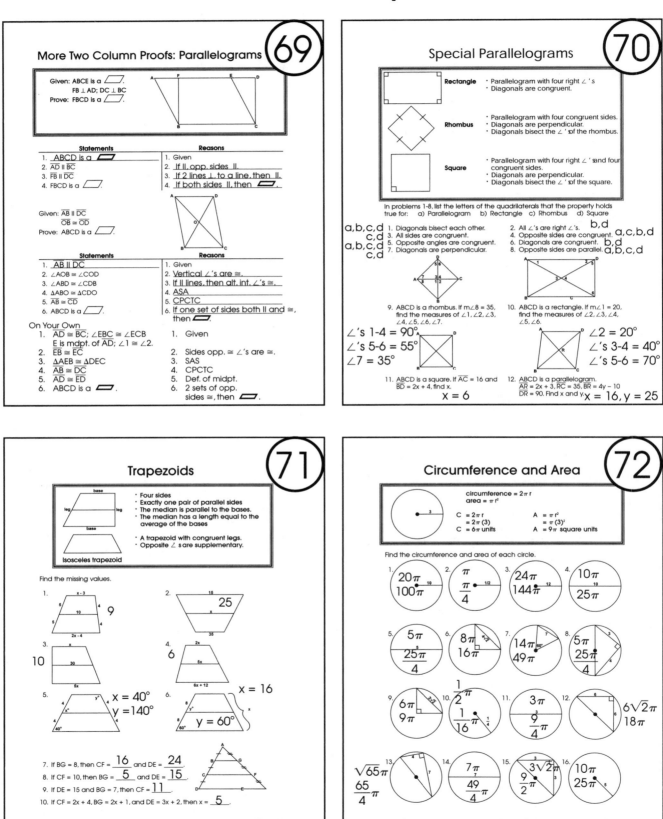

69 More Two Column Proofs: Parallelograms

Given: ABCE is a ▱.
FB ⊥ AD; DC ⊥ BC
Prove: FBCD is a ▱.

Statements	Reasons
1. ABCD is a ▱	1. Given
2. $\overline{AD} \parallel \overline{BC}$	2. If ▱, opp. sides ∥.
3. $\overline{FB} \parallel \overline{DC}$	3. If 2 lines ⊥ to a line, then ∥.
4. FBCD is a ▱.	4. If both sides ∥, then ▱.

Given: $\overline{AB} \parallel \overline{DC}$
$\overline{OB} \cong \overline{OD}$
Prove: ABCD is a ▱.

Statements	Reasons
1. $\overline{AB} \parallel \overline{DC}$	1. Given
2. ∠AOB ≅ ∠COD	2. Vertical ∠'s are ≅.
3. ∠ABD ≅ ∠CDB	3. If ∥ lines, then alt. int. ∠'s ≅.
4. △ABO ≅ △CDO	4. ASA
5. $\overline{AB} \cong \overline{CD}$	5. CPCTC
6. ABCD is a ▱.	6. If one set of sides both ∥ and ≅, then ▱.

On Your Own

1. $\overline{AD} \cong \overline{BC}$; ∠EBC ≅ ∠ECB E is mdpt. of $\overline{AD}$; ∠1 ≅ ∠2.	1. Given
2. $\overline{EB} \cong \overline{EC}$	2. Sides opp. ≅ ∠'s are ≅.
3. △AEB ≅ △DEC	3. SAS
4. $\overline{AB} \cong \overline{DC}$	4. CPCTC
5. $\overline{AD} \cong \overline{ED}$	5. Def. of midpt.
6. ABCD is a ▱.	6. 2 sets of opp. sides ≅, then ▱.

70 Special Parallelograms

Rectangle
· Parallelogram with four right ∠'s
· Diagonals are congruent.

Rhombus
· Parallelogram with four congruent sides.
· Diagonals are perpendicular.
· Diagonals bisect the ∠'s of the rhombus.

Square
· Parallelogram with four right ∠'s and four congruent sides.
· Diagonals are perpendicular.
· Diagonals bisect the ∠'s of the square.

In problems 1-8, list the letters of the quadrilaterals that the property holds true for: a) Parallelogram   b) Rectangle   c) Rhombus   d) Square

a,b,c,d 1. Diagonals bisect each other.   2. All ∠'s are right ∠'s. b,d
c,d 3. All sides are congruent.   4. Opposite sides are congruent. a,c,b,d
a,b,c,d 5. Opposite angles are congruent.   6. Diagonals are congruent. b,d
c,d 7. Diagonals are perpendicular.   8. Opposite sides are parallel. a,b,c,d

9. ABCD is a rhombus. If m∠8 = 35, find the measures of ∠1, ∠2, ∠3, ∠4, ∠5, ∠6, ∠7.

∠'s 1-4 = 90°
∠'s 5-6 = 55°
∠7 = 35°

10. ABCD is a rectangle. If m∠1 = 20, find the measures of ∠2, ∠3, ∠4, ∠5, ∠6.

∠2 = 20°
∠'s 3-4 = 40°
∠'s 5-6 = 70°

11. ABCD is a square. If $\overline{AC}$ = 16 and $\overline{BD}$ = 2x + 4, find x.

x = 6

12. ABCD is a parallelogram. $\overline{AR}$ = 2x + 3, $\overline{RC}$ = 35, $\overline{BR}$ = 4y − 10 $\overline{DR}$ = 90. Find x and y. x = 16, y = 25

71 Trapezoids

· Four sides
· Exactly one pair of parallel sides.
· The median is parallel to the bases.
· The median has a length equal to the average of the bases

· A trapezoid with congruent legs.
· Opposite ∠'s are supplementary.

Isosceles trapezoid

Find the missing values.

1. 9
2. 25
3. 10
4. 6
5. x = 40° y = 140°
6. x = 16 y = 60°

7. If BG = 8, then CF = **16** and DE = **24**.
8. If CF = 10, then BG = **5** and DE = **15**.
9. If DE = 15 and BG = 7, then CF = **11**.
10. If CF = 2x + 4, BG = 2x + 1, and DE = 3x + 2, then x = **5**.

72 Circumference and Area

circumference = 2π r
area = π r²

C = 2π r   A = π r²
  = 2π (3)   = π (3)²
C = 6π units   A = 9π square units

Find the circumference and area of each circle.

1. 20π / 100π
2. π / π/4
3. 24π / 144π
4. 10π / 25π
5. 5π / 25π/4
6. 8π / 16π
7. 14π / 49π
8. 5π / 25π/4
9. 6π / 9π
10. 1/2 π / 1/16 π
11. 3π / 9/4 π
12. 6√2 π / 18π
13. √65 π / 65/4 π
14. 7π / 49/4 π
15. 3√2 π / 9/2 π
16. 10π / 25π

Answer Key

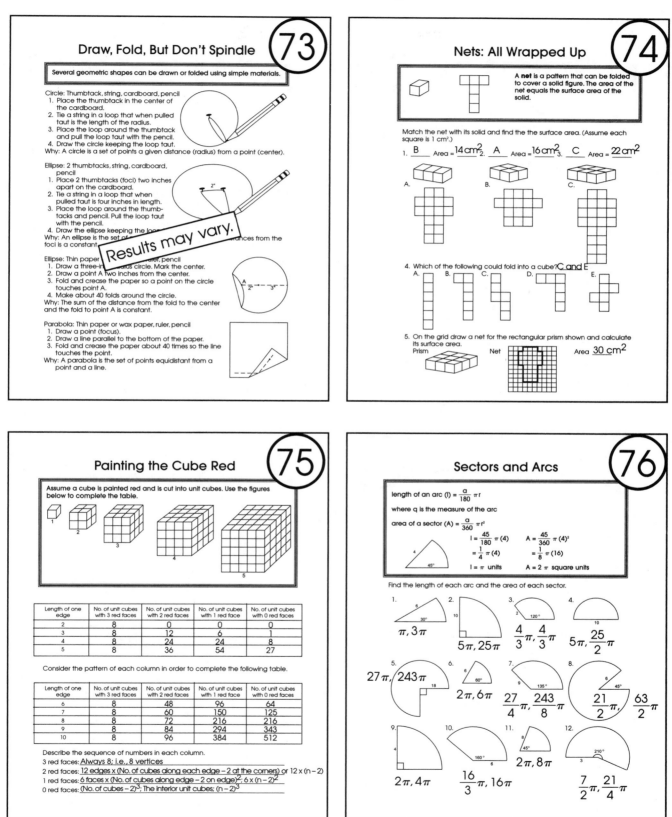

Draw, Fold, But Don't Spindle — 73

Several geometric shapes can be drawn or folded using simple materials.

Circle: Thumbtack, string, cardboard, pencil
1. Place the thumbtack in the center of the cardboard.
2. Tie a string in a loop that when pulled taut is the length of the radius.
3. Place the loop around the thumbtack and pull the loop taut with the pencil.
4. Draw the circle keeping the loop taut.
Why: A circle is a set of points a given distance (radius) from a point (center).

Ellipse: 2 thumbtacks, string, cardboard, pencil
1. Place 2 thumbtacks (foci) two inches apart on the cardboard.
2. Tie a string in a loop that when pulled taut is four inches in length.
3. Place the loop around the thumbtacks and pencil. Pull the loop taut with the pencil.
4. Draw the ellipse keeping the loop taut.
Why: An ellipse is the set of points whose sum of the distances from the foci is a constant.

Ellipse: Thin paper, compass, ruler, pencil
1. Draw a three-inch radius circle. Mark the center.
2. Draw a point A two inches from the center.
3. Fold and crease the paper so a point on the circle touches point A.
4. Make about 40 folds around the circle.
Why: The sum of the distance from the fold to the center and the fold to point A is constant.

Parabola: Thin paper or wax paper, ruler, pencil
1. Draw a point (focus).
2. Draw a line parallel to the bottom of the paper.
3. Fold and crease the paper about 40 times so the line touches the point.
Why: A parabola is the set of points equidistant from a point and a line.

Results may vary.

Nets: All Wrapped Up — 74

A **net** is a pattern that can be folded to cover a solid figure. The area of the net equals the surface area of the solid.

Match the net with its solid and find the the surface area. (Assume each square is 1 cm².)

1. __B__ Area = 14 cm² 2. __A__ Area = 16 cm² 3. __C__ Area = 22 cm²

4. Which of the following could fold into a cube? __C and E__

5. On the grid draw a net for the rectangular prism shown and calculate its surface area.
Prism   Net   Area __30__ cm²

Painting the Cube Red — 75

Assume a cube is painted red and is cut into unit cubes. Use the figures below to complete the table.

Length of one edge	No. of unit cubes with 3 red faces	No. of unit cubes with 2 red faces	No. of unit cubes with 1 red face	No. of unit cubes with 0 red faces
2	8	0	0	0
3	8	12	6	1
4	8	24	24	8
5	8	36	54	27

Consider the pattern of each column in order to complete the following table.

Length of one edge	No. of unit cubes with 3 red faces	No. of unit cubes with 2 red faces	No. of unit cubes with 1 red face	No. of unit cubes with 0 red faces
6	8	48	96	64
7	8	60	150	125
8	8	72	216	216
9	8	84	294	343
10	8	96	384	512

Describe the sequence of numbers in each column.
3 red faces: Always 8; i.e., 8 vertices
2 red faces: 12 edges x (No. of cubes along each edge – 2 at the corners) or 12 x (n – 2)
1 red faces: 6 faces x (No. of cubes along edge – 2 on edge)²; 6 x (n – 2)²
0 red faces: (No. of cubes – 2)³; The interior unit cubes; (n – 2)³

Sectors and Arcs — 76

length of an arc (l) = $\frac{a}{180}\pi r$

where q is the measure of the arc

area of a sector (A) = $\frac{a}{360}\pi r^2$

$l = \frac{45}{180}\pi(4)$ $A = \frac{45}{360}\pi(4)^2$

$= \frac{1}{4}\pi(4)$ $= \frac{1}{8}\pi(16)$

$l = \pi$ units $A = 2\pi$ square units

Find the length of each arc and the area of each sector.

1. $\pi, 3\pi$

2. $5\pi, 25\pi$

3. $\frac{4}{3}\pi, \frac{4}{3}\pi$

4. $5\pi, \frac{25}{2}\pi$

5. $27\pi, 243\pi$

6. $2\pi, 6\pi$

7. $\frac{27}{4}\pi, \frac{243}{8}\pi$

8. $\frac{21}{2}\pi, \frac{63}{2}\pi$

9. $2\pi, 4\pi$

10. $\frac{16}{3}\pi, 16\pi$

11. $2\pi, 8\pi$

12. $\frac{7}{2}\pi, \frac{21}{4}\pi$

0-7424-1776-X *Geometry*

Answer Key

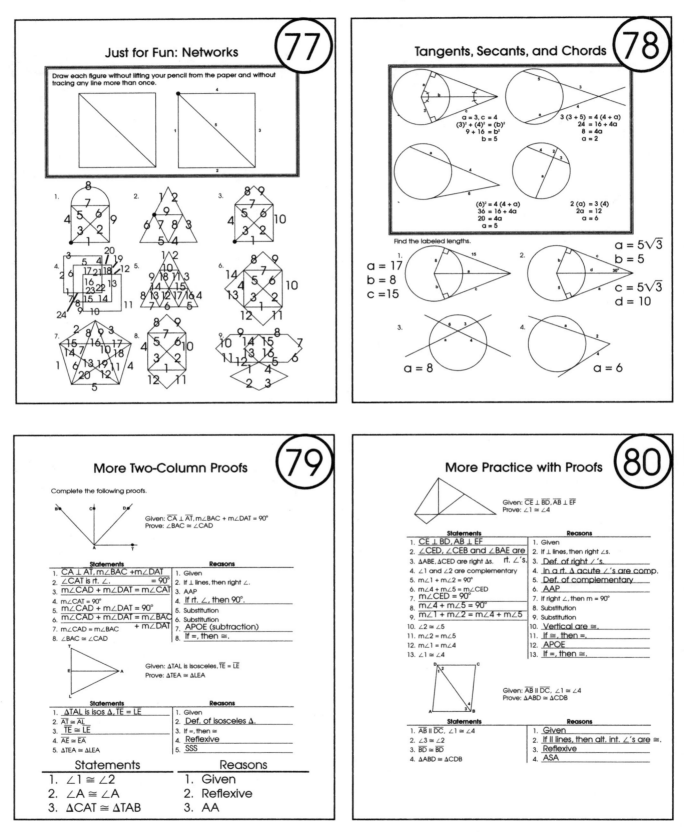

Just for Fun: Networks (77)

Draw each figure without lifting your pencil from the paper and without tracing any line more than once.

Tangents, Secants, and Chords (78)

$a = 3, c = 4$
$(3)^2 + (4)^2 = (b)^2$
$9 + 16 = b^2$
$b = 5$

$3 (3 + 5) = 4 (4 + a)$
$24 = 16 + 4a$
$8 = 4a$
$a = 2$

$(6)^2 = 4 (4 + a)$
$36 = 16 + 4a$
$20 = 4a$
$a = 5$

$2 (a) = 3 (4)$
$2a = 12$
$a = 6$

Find the labeled lengths.

1. $a = 17$ $b = 8$ $c = 15$

2. $a = 5\sqrt{3}$ $b = 5$ $c = 5\sqrt{3}$ $d = 10$

3. $a = 8$

4. $a = 6$

More Two-Column Proofs (79)

Complete the following proofs.

Given: $\overline{CA} \perp \overline{AT}, m\angle BAC + m\angle DAT = 90°$
Prove: $\angle BAC \cong \angle CAD$

Statements	Reasons
1. $CA \perp AT, m\angle BAC + m\angle DAT = 90°$	1. Given
2. $\angle CAT$ is rt. $\angle$.	2. If $\perp$ lines, then right $\angle$.
3. $m\angle CAD + m\angle DAT = m\angle CAT$	3. AAP
4. $m\angle CAT = 90°$	4. If rt. $\angle$, then 90°.
5. $m\angle CAD + m\angle DAT = 90°$	5. Substitution
6. $m\angle CAD + m\angle DAT = m\angle BAC + m\angle DAT$	6. Substitution
7. $m\angle CAD = m\angle BAC$	7. APOE (subtraction)
8. $\angle BAC \cong \angle CAD$	8. If =, then $\cong$.

Given: $\triangle TAL$ is isosceles, $\overline{TE} = \overline{LE}$
Prove: $\triangle TEA \cong \triangle LEA$

Statements	Reasons
1. $\triangle TAL$ is isos $\triangle$, $TE = LE$	1. Given
2. $\overline{AT} \cong \overline{AL}$	2. Def. of isosceles $\triangle$.
3. $\overline{TE} \cong \overline{LE}$	3. If =, then $\cong$.
4. $\overline{AE} \cong \overline{EA}$	4. Reflexive
5. $\triangle TEA \cong \triangle LEA$	5. SSS

Statements	Reasons
1. $\angle 1 \cong \angle 2$	1. Given
2. $\angle A \cong \angle A$	2. Reflexive
3. $\triangle CAT \cong \triangle TAB$	3. AA

More Practice with Proofs (80)

Given: $\overline{CE} \perp \overline{BD}, \overline{AB} \perp \overline{EF}$
Prove: $\angle 1 \cong \angle 4$

Statements	Reasons
1. $CE \perp BD, AB \perp EF$	1. Given
2. $\angle CED, \angle CEB$ and $\angle BAE$ are rt. $\angle$'s.	2. If $\perp$ lines, then right $\angle$s.
3. $\triangle ABE, \triangle CED$ are right $\triangle$s.	3. Def. of right $\angle$'s.
4. $\angle 1$ and $\angle 2$ are complementary	4. In a rt. $\triangle$ acute $\angle$'s are comp.
5. $m\angle 1 + m\angle 2 = 90°$	5. Def. of complementary
6. $m\angle 4 + m\angle 5 = m\angle CED$	6. AAP
7. $m\angle CED = 90°$	7. If right $\angle$, then m = 90°
8. $m\angle 4 + m\angle 5 = 90°$	8. Substitution
9. $m\angle 1 + m\angle 2 = m\angle 4 + m\angle 5$	9. Substitution
10. $\angle 2 \cong \angle 5$	10. Vertical are $\cong$.
11. $m\angle 2 = m\angle 5$	11. If $\cong$, then =,
12. $m\angle 1 = m\angle 4$	12. APOE
13. $\angle 1 \cong \angle 4$	13. If =, then $\cong$.

Given: $\overline{AB} \parallel \overline{DC}, \angle 1 \cong \angle 4$
Prove: $\triangle ABD \cong \triangle CDB$

Statements	Reasons
1. $\overline{AB} \parallel \overline{DC}, \angle 1 \cong \angle 4$	1. Given
2. $\angle 3 \cong \angle 2$	2. If $\parallel$ lines, then alt. int. $\angle$'s are $\cong$.
3. $\overline{BD} \cong \overline{BD}$	3. Reflexive
4. $\triangle ABD \cong \triangle CDB$	4. ASA

0-7424-1776-X Geometry

Answer Key

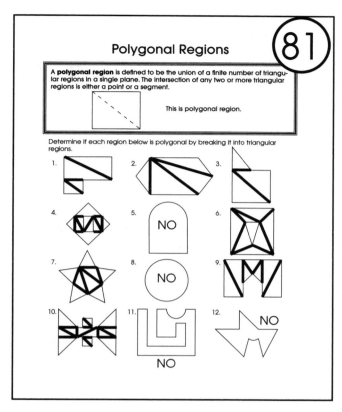

Polygonal Regions (81)

A **polygonal region** is defined to be the union of a finite number of triangular regions in a single plane. The intersection of any two or more triangular regions is either a point or a segment.

This is polygonal region.

Determine if each region below is polygonal by breaking it into triangular regions.

1.   2.   3.

4.   5. NO   6.

7.   8. NO   9.

10.   11. NO   12. NO

Polygons (82)

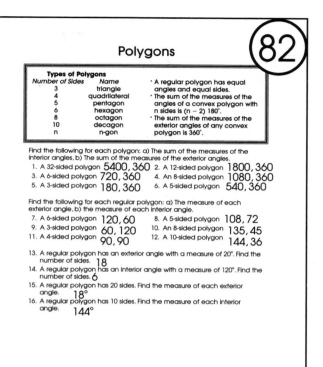

Types of Polygons

Number of Sides	Name
3	triangle
4	quadrilateral
5	pentagon
6	hexagon
8	octagon
10	decagon
n	n-gon

- A regular polygon has equal angles and equal sides.
- The sum of the measures of the angles of a convex polygon with n sides is $(n - 2)\,180°$.
- The sum of the measures of the exterior angles of any convex polygon is $360°$.

Find the following for each polygon: a) The sum of the measures of the interior angles, b) The sum of the measures of the exterior angles.
1. A 32-sided polygon **5400, 360**   2. A 12-sided polygon **1800, 360**
3. A 6-sided polygon **720, 360**   4. An 8-sided polygon **1080, 360**
5. A 3-sided polygon **180, 360**   6. A 5-sided polygon **540, 360**

Find the following for each regular polygon: a) The measure of each exterior angle, b) the measure of each interior angle.
7. A 6-sided polygon **120, 60**   8. A 5-sided polygon **108, 72**
9. A 3-sided polygon **60, 120**   10. An 8-sided polygon **135, 45**
11. A 4-sided polygon **90, 90**   12. A 10-sided polygon **144, 36**

13. A regular polygon has an exterior angle with a measure of 20°. Find the number of sides. **18**
14. A regular polygon has an interior angle with a measure of 120°. Find the number of sides. **6**
15. A regular polygon has 20 sides. Find the measure of each exterior angle. **18°**
16. A regular polygon has 10 sides. Find the measure of each interior angle. **144°**

Perimeter (83)

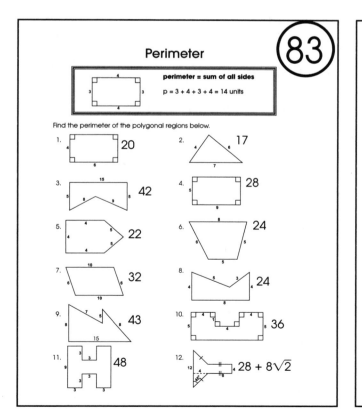

perimeter = sum of all sides

$p = 3 + 4 + 3 + 4 = 14$ units

Find the perimeter of the polygonal regions below.

1. **20**   2. **17**
3. **42**   4. **28**
5. **22**   6. **24**
7. **32**   8. **24**
9. **43**   10. **36**
11. **48**   12. **$28 + 8\sqrt{2}$**

Area (84)

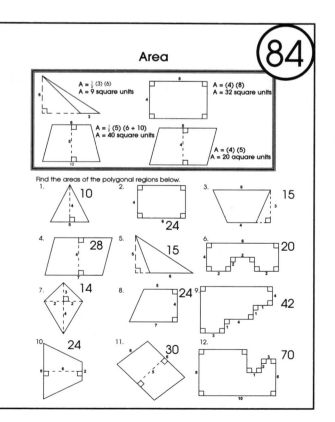

$A = \frac{1}{2}(3)(6)$
$A = 9$ square units

$A = (4)(8)$
$A = 32$ square units

$A = \frac{1}{2}(5)(6 + 10)$
$A = 40$ square units

$A = (4)(5)$
$A = 20$ square units

Find the areas of the polygonal regions below.

1. **10**   2. **24**   3. **15**
4. **28**   5. **15**   6. **20**
7. **14**   8. **24**   9. **42**
10. **24**   11. **30**   12. **70**

0-7424-1776-X *Geometry*

Answer Key

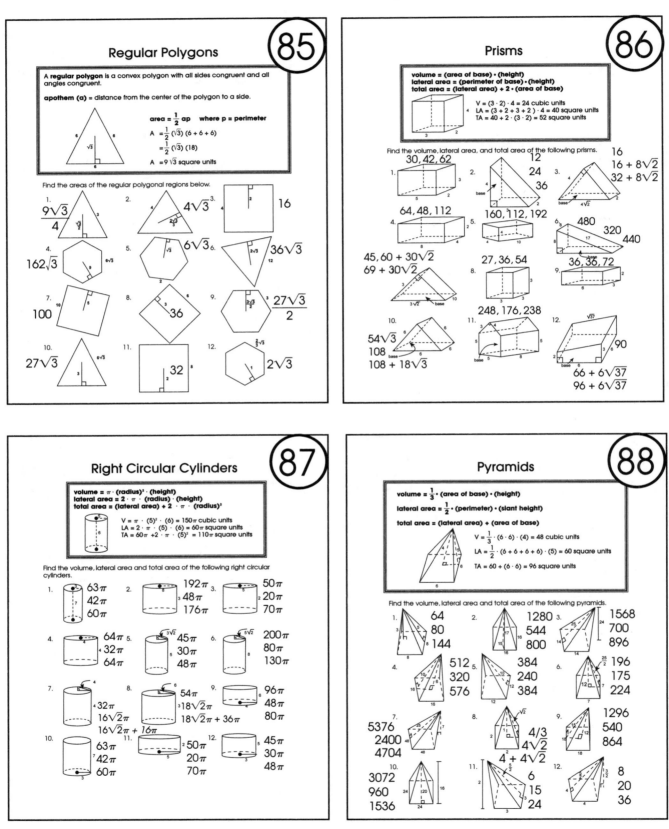

Regular Polygons ⑧⑤

A **regular polygon** is a convex polygon with all sides congruent and all angles congruent.

apothem (a) = distance from the center of the polygon to a side.

area = $\frac{1}{2}$ ap   where p = perimeter

$A = \frac{1}{2}(\sqrt{3})(6 + 6 + 6)$
$= \frac{1}{2}(\sqrt{3})(18)$
$A = 9\sqrt{3}$ square units

Find the areas of the regular polygonal regions below.

1. $\frac{9\sqrt{3}}{4}$ 2. $4\sqrt{3}$ 3. 16

4. $162\sqrt{3}$ 5. $6\sqrt{3}$ 6. $36\sqrt{3}$

7. 100 8. 36 9. $\frac{27\sqrt{3}}{2}$

10. $27\sqrt{3}$ 11. 32 12. $2\sqrt{3}$

Prisms ⑧⑥

volume = (area of base) • (height)
lateral area = (perimeter of base) • (height)
total area = (lateral area) + 2 • (area of base)

$V = (3 \cdot 2) \cdot 4 = 24$ cubic units
$LA = (3 + 2 + 3 + 2) \cdot 4 = 40$ square units
$TA = 40 + 2 \cdot (3 \cdot 2) = 52$ square units

Find the volume, lateral area, and total area of the following prisms.

1. $30, 42, 62$ 2. $12, 24, 36$ 3. $16, 16 + 8\sqrt{2}, 32 + 8\sqrt{2}$

4. $64, 48, 112$ 5. $160, 112, 192$ 6. $480, 320, 440$

7. $45, 60 + 30\sqrt{2}, 69 + 30\sqrt{2}$ 8. $27, 36, 54$ 9. $36, 36, 72$

10. $54\sqrt{3}, 108, 108 + 18\sqrt{3}$ 11. $248, 176, 238$ 12. $90, 66 + 6\sqrt{37}, 96 + 6\sqrt{37}$

Right Circular Cylinders ⑧⑦

volume = π • (radius)² • (height)
lateral area = 2 • π • (radius) • (height)
total area = (lateral area) + 2 • π • (radius)²

$V = \pi \cdot (5)^2 \cdot (6) = 150\pi$ cubic units
$LA = 2 \cdot \pi \cdot (5) \cdot (6) = 60\pi$ square units
$TA = 60\pi + 2 \cdot \pi \cdot (5)^2 = 110\pi$ square units

Find the volume, lateral area and total area of the following right circular cylinders.

1. $63\pi, 42\pi, 60\pi$ 2. $192\pi, 48\pi, 176\pi$ 3. $50\pi, 20\pi, 70\pi$

4. $64\pi, 32\pi, 64\pi$ 5. $45\pi, 30\pi, 48\pi$ 6. $200\pi, 80\pi, 130\pi$

7. $32\pi, 16\sqrt{2}\pi, 16\sqrt{2}\pi + 16\pi$ 8. $54\pi, 18\sqrt{2}\pi, 18\sqrt{2}\pi + 36\pi$ 9. $96\pi, 48\pi, 80\pi$

10. $63\pi, 42\pi, 60\pi$ 11. $50\pi, 20\pi, 70\pi$ 12. $45\pi, 30\pi, 48\pi$

Pyramids ⑧⑧

volume = $\frac{1}{3}$ • (area of base) • (height)

lateral area = $\frac{1}{2}$ • (perimeter) • (slant height)

total area = (lateral area) + (area of base)

$V = \frac{1}{3} \cdot (6 \cdot 6) \cdot (4) = 48$ cubic units
$LA = \frac{1}{2} \cdot (6 + 6 + 6 + 6) \cdot (5) = 60$ square units
$TA = 60 + (6 \cdot 6) = 96$ square units

Find the volume, lateral area and total area of the following pyramids.

1. $64, 80, 144$ 2. $1280, 544, 800$ 3. $1568, 700, 896$

4. $512, 320, 576$ 5. $384, 240, 384$ 6. $196, 175, 224$

7. $5376, 2400, 4704$ 8. $4/3, 4\sqrt{2}, 4 + 4\sqrt{2}$ 9. $1296, 540, 864$

10. $3072, 960, 1536$ 11. $6, 15, 24$ 12. $8, 20, 36$

Answer Key

Right Circular Cones — 89

volume = $\frac{1}{3} \cdot \pi \cdot$ (radius)$^2 \cdot$ (height)

lateral area = $\pi \cdot$ (radius) $\cdot$ (slant height)

total area = (lateral area) + $\pi \cdot$ (radius)^2

$V = \frac{1}{3} \cdot \pi \cdot (3)^2 \cdot (4) = 12\pi$ cubic units

$LA = \pi \cdot (3) \cdot (5) = 15\pi$ square units

$TA = 15\pi + 15\pi \cdot (3)^2 = 24\pi$ square units

Find the volume, lateral area and total area of the following right circular cones.

1. 320π / 136π / 200π

2. 16π / 20π / 36π

3. $2/3\pi$ / $\sqrt5\pi$ / $(1 + \sqrt5)\pi$

4. $8/3\pi$ / $4\sqrt2\pi$ / $4\pi + 4\sqrt2\pi$

5. 96π / 60π / 96π

6. 392π / 175π / 224π

7. 9π / $9\sqrt2\pi$ / $9\pi + 9\sqrt2\pi$

8. 324π / 135π / 216π

9. 18π / $9\sqrt5\pi$ / $9\pi + 9\sqrt5\pi$

10. 2560π / 544π / 800π

11. $\frac{1}{3}\pi$ / $\sqrt2\pi$ / $1\pi + \sqrt2\pi$

12. 128π / 80π / 144π

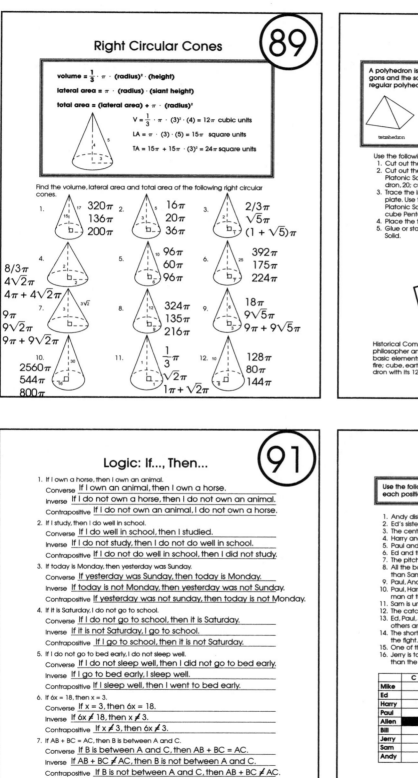

Platonic Solids — 90

A polyhedron is **regular** if all faces of the solid are congruent regular polygons and the same number of polygons meet at each vertex. There are only 5 regular polyhedra—the Platonic Solids.

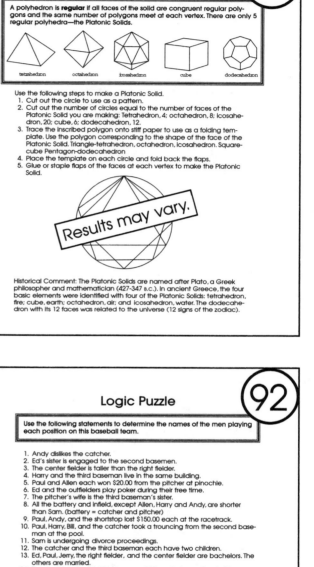

tetrahedron   octahedron   icosahedron   cube   dodecahedron

Use the following steps to make a Platonic Solid.
1. Cut out the circle to use as a pattern.
2. Cut out the number of circles equal to the number of faces of the Platonic Solid you are making: Tetrahedron, 4; octahedron, 8; icosahedron, 20; cube, 6; dodecahedron, 12.
3. Trace the inscribed polygon onto stiff paper to use as a folding template. Use the polygon corresponding to the shape of the face of the Platonic Solid. Triangle-tetrahedron, octahedron, icosahedron. Square-cube Pentagon-dodecahedron
4. Place the template on each circle and fold back the flaps.
5. Glue or staple flaps of the faces at each vertex to make the Platonic Solid.

Results may vary.

Historical Comment: The Platonic Solids are named after Plato, a Greek philosopher and mathematician (427-347 B.C.). In ancient Greece, the four basic elements were identified with four of the Platonic Solids: tetrahedron, fire; cube, earth; octahedron, air; and icosahedron, water. The dodecahedron with its 12 faces was related to the universe (12 signs of the zodiac).

Logic: If..., Then... — 91

1. If I own a horse, then I own an animal.
   Converse: If I own an animal, then I own a horse.
   Inverse: If I do not own a horse, then I do not own an animal.
   Contrapositive: If I do not own an animal, I do not own a horse.

2. If I study, then I do well in school.
   Converse: If I do well in school, then I studied.
   Inverse: If I do not study, then I do not do well in school.
   Contrapositive: If I do not do well in school, then I did not study.

3. If today is Monday, then yesterday was Sunday.
   Converse: If yesterday was Sunday, then today is Monday.
   Inverse: If today is not Monday, then yesterday was not Sunday.
   Contrapositive: If yesterday was not sunday, then today is not Monday.

4. If it is Saturday, I do not go to school.
   Converse: If I do not go to school, then it is Saturday.
   Inverse: If it is not Saturday, I go to school.
   Contrapositive: If I go to school, then it is not Saturday.

5. If I do not go to bed early, I do not sleep well.
   Converse: If I do not sleep well, then I did not go to bed early.
   Inverse: If I go to bed early, I sleep well.
   Contrapositive: If I sleep well, then I went to bed early.

6. If $6x = 18$, then $x = 3$.
   Converse: If $x = 3$, then $6x = 18$.
   Inverse: If $6x \neq 18$, then $x \neq 3$.
   Contrapositive: If $x \neq 3$, then $6x \neq 3$.

7. If $AB + BC = AC$, then B is between A and C.
   Converse: If B is between A and C, then $AB + BC = AC$.
   Inverse: If $AB + BC \neq AC$, then B is not between A and C.
   Contrapositive: If B is not between A and C, then $AB + BC \neq AC$.

8. Given a conditional statement, the __contrapositive__ statement is **always** true.
   Choose from converse, inverse, or contrapositive.)

Logic Puzzle — 92

Use the following statements to determine the names of the men playing each position on this baseball team.

1. Andy dislikes the catcher.
2. Ed's sister is engaged to the second basemen.
3. The center fielder is taller than the right fielder.
4. Harry and the third baseman live in the same building.
5. Paul and Allen each won $20.00 from the pitcher at pinochle.
6. Ed and the outfielders play poker during their free time.
7. The pitcher's wife is the third baseman's sister.
8. All the battery and infield, except Allen, Harry and Andy, are shorter than Sam. (battery = catcher and pitcher)
9. Paul, Andy, and the shortstop lost $150.00 each at the racetrack.
10. Paul, Harry, Bill, and the catcher took a trouncing from the second baseman at the pool.
11. Sam is undergoing divorce proceedings.
12. The catcher and the third baseman each have two children.
13. Ed, Paul, Jerry, the right fielder, and the center fielder are bachelors. The others are married.
14. The shortstop, the third baseman and Bill each cleaned up betting on the fight.
15. One of the outfielders is either Mike or Andy.
16. Jerry is taller than Bill. Mike is shorter than Bill. Each of them is heavier than the third baseman.

	C	P	SS	1st	2nd	3rd	LF	CF	RF
Mike									■
Ed			■						
Harry	■								
Paul					■				
Allen	■								
Bill							■		
Jerry					■				
Sam						■			
Andy						■			

Answer Key

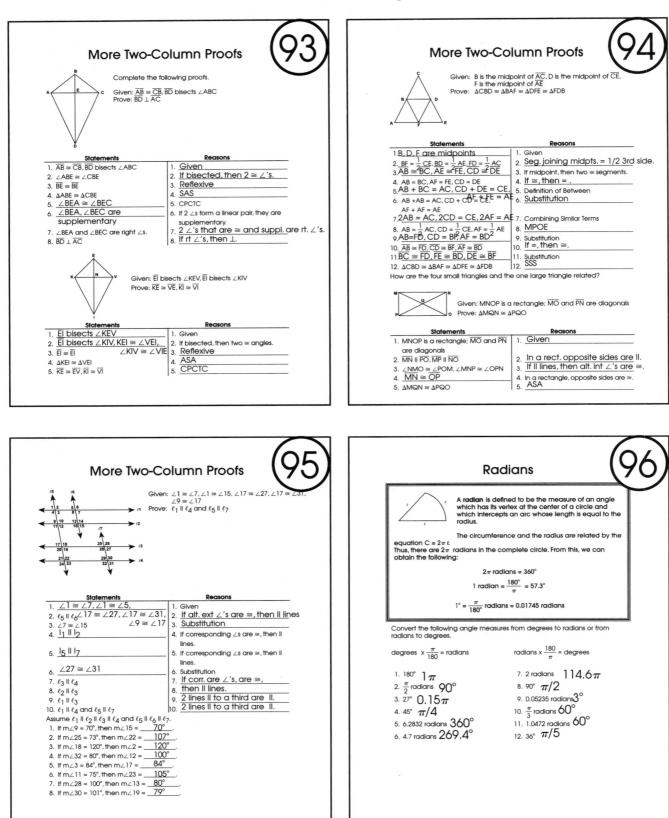

93 — More Two-Column Proofs

Complete the following proofs.

Given: $\overline{AB} \cong \overline{CB}$, $\overline{BD}$ bisects $\angle ABC$
Prove: $\overline{BD} \perp \overline{AC}$

Statements	Reasons
1. $\overline{AB} \cong \overline{CB}$, $\overline{BD}$ bisects $\angle ABC$	1. Given
2. $\angle ABE \cong \angle CBE$	2. If bisected, then 2 $\cong$ $\angle$'s.
3. $\overline{BE} \cong \overline{BE}$	3. Reflexive
4. $\triangle ABE \cong \triangle CBE$	4. SAS
5. $\angle BEA \cong \angle BEC$	5. CPCTC
6. $\angle BEA$, $\angle BEC$ are supplementary	6. If 2 $\angle$s form a linear pair, they are supplementary.
7. $\angle BEA$ and $\angle BEC$ are right $\angle$s.	7. 2 $\angle$'s that are $\cong$ and suppl. are rt. $\angle$'s.
8. $\overline{BD} \perp \overline{AC}$	8. If rt $\angle$'s, then $\perp$.

Given: $\overline{EI}$ bisects $\angle KEV$, $\overline{EI}$ bisects $\angle KIV$
Prove: $\overline{KE} \cong \overline{VE}$, $\overline{KI} \cong \overline{VI}$

Statements	Reasons
1. $\overline{EI}$ bisects $\angle KEV$	1. Given
2. $\overline{EI}$ bisects $\angle KIV$, $KEI \cong \angle VEI$, $\angle KIV \cong \angle VIE$	2. If bisected, then two $\cong$ angles.
3. $\overline{EI} \cong \overline{EI}$	3. Reflexive
4. $\triangle KEI \cong \triangle VEI$	4. ASA
5. $\overline{KE} \cong \overline{EV}$, $\overline{KI} \cong \overline{VI}$	5. CPCTC

94 — More Two-Column Proofs

Given: B is the midpoint of $\overline{AC}$, D is the midpoint of $\overline{CE}$,
F is the midpoint of $\overline{AE}$
Prove: $\triangle CBD \cong \triangle BAF \cong \triangle DFE \cong \triangle FDB$

Statements	Reasons
1. B, D, F are midpoints	1. Given
2. $BF = \frac{1}{2}CE$, $BD = \frac{1}{2}AE$, $FD = \frac{1}{2}AC$	2. Seg. joining midpts. = 1/2 3rd side.
3. $\overline{AB} \cong \overline{BC}$, $\overline{AE} \cong \overline{FE}$, $\overline{CD} \cong \overline{DE}$	3. If midpoint, then two $\cong$ segments.
4. $AB = BC$, $AF = FE$, $CD = DE$	4. If $\cong$, then $=$.
5. $AB + BC = AC$, $CD + DE = CE$, $AF + FE = AE$	5. Definition of Between
6. $AB + AB = AC$, $CD + CD = CE$, $AF + AF = AE$	6. Substitution
7. $2AB = AC$, $2CD = CE$, $2AF = AE$	7. Combining Similar Terms
8. $AB = \frac{1}{2}AC$, $CD = \frac{1}{2}CE$, $AF = \frac{1}{2}AE$	8. MPOE
9. $AB = FD$, $CD = BF$, $AF = BD$	9. Substitution
10. $\overline{AB} \cong \overline{FD}$, $\overline{CD} \cong \overline{BF}$, $\overline{AF} \cong \overline{BD}$	10. If $=$, then $\cong$.
11. $\overline{BC} \cong \overline{FD}$, $\overline{FE} \cong \overline{BD}$, $\overline{DE} \cong \overline{BF}$	11. Substitution
12. $\triangle CBD \cong \triangle BAF \cong \triangle DFE \cong \triangle FDB$	12. SSS

How are the four small triangles and the one large triangle related?

Given: MNOP is a rectangle; $\overline{MO}$ and $\overline{PN}$ are diagonals
Prove: $\triangle MQN \cong \triangle PQO$

Statements	Reasons
1. MNOP is a rectangle; $\overline{MO}$ and $\overline{PN}$ are diagonals	1. Given
2. $\overline{MN} \parallel \overline{PO}$, $\overline{MP} \parallel \overline{NO}$	2. In a rect. opposite sides are $\parallel$.
3. $\angle NMO \cong \angle POM$, $\angle MNP \cong \angle OPN$	3. If $\parallel$ lines, then alt. int $\angle$'s are $\cong$.
4. $\overline{MN} \cong \overline{OP}$	4. In a rectangle, opposite sides are $\cong$.
5. $\triangle MQN \cong \triangle PQO$	5. ASA

95 — More Two-Column Proofs

Given: $\angle 1 \cong \angle 7$, $\angle 1 \cong \angle 15$, $\angle 17 \cong \angle 27$, $\angle 17 \cong \angle 31$, $\angle 9 \cong \angle 17$
Prove: $\ell_1 \parallel \ell_4$ and $\ell_5 \parallel \ell_7$

Statements	Reasons
1. $\angle 1 \cong \angle 7$, $\angle 1 \cong \angle 5$,	1. Given
2. $\ell_5 \parallel \ell_6$, $\angle 17 \cong \angle 27$, $\angle 17 \cong \angle 31$,	2. If alt. ext $\angle$'s are $\cong$, then $\parallel$ lines
3. $\angle 7 \cong \angle 15$, $\angle 9 \cong \angle 17$	3. Substitution
4. $\ell_1 \parallel \ell_2$	4. If corresponding $\angle$s are $\cong$, then $\parallel$ lines.
5. $\ell_5 \parallel \ell_7$	5. If corresponding $\angle$s are $\cong$, then $\parallel$ lines.
6. $\angle 27 \cong \angle 31$	6. Substitution
7. $\ell_3 \parallel \ell_4$	7. If corr. are $\angle$'s, are $\cong$, then $\parallel$ lines.
8. $\ell_2 \parallel \ell_3$	8. then $\parallel$ lines.
9. $\ell_1 \parallel \ell_3$	9. 2 lines $\parallel$ to a third are $\parallel$.
10. $\ell_1 \parallel \ell_4$ and $\ell_5 \parallel \ell_7$	10. 2 lines $\parallel$ to a third are $\parallel$.

Assume $\ell_1 \parallel \ell_2 \parallel \ell_3 \parallel \ell_4$ and $\ell_5 \parallel \ell_6 \parallel \ell_7$.

1. If $m\angle 9 = 70°$, then $m\angle 15 = $ __70°__
2. If $m\angle 25 = 73°$, then $m\angle 22 = $ __107°__
3. If $m\angle 18 = 120°$, then $m\angle 2 = $ __120°__
4. If $m\angle 32 = 80°$, then $m\angle 12 = $ __100°__
5. If $m\angle 3 = 84°$, then $m\angle 17 = $ __84°__
6. If $m\angle 11 = 75°$, then $m\angle 23 = $ __105°__
7. If $m\angle 28 = 100°$, then $m\angle 13 = $ __80°__
8. If $m\angle 30 = 101°$, then $m\angle 19 = $ __79°__

96 — Radians

A **radian** is defined to be the measure of an angle which has its vertex at the center of a circle and which intercepts an arc whose length is equal to the radius.

The circumference and the radius are related by the equation $C = 2\pi r$.
Thus, there are 2π radians in the complete circle. From this, we can obtain the following:

$$2\pi \text{ radians} = 360°$$

$$1 \text{ radian} = \frac{180°}{\pi} = 57.3°$$

$$1° = \frac{\pi}{180°} \text{ radians} = 0.01745 \text{ radians}$$

Convert the following angle measures from degrees to radians or from radians to degrees.

degrees $\times \frac{\pi}{180}$ = radians   radians $\times \frac{180}{\pi}$ = degrees

1. 180° __1π__
2. $\frac{\pi}{2}$ radians __90°__
3. 27° __0.15π__
4. 45° __$\pi/4$__
5. 6.2832 radians __360°__
6. 4.7 radians __269.4°__
7. 2 radians __114.6π__
8. 90° __$\pi/2$__
9. 0.05235 radians __3°__
10. $\frac{\pi}{3}$ radians __60°__
11. 1.0472 radians __60°__
12. 36° __$\pi/5$__